Macmillar

CW00457362

A 102-mile Footpa
from
being an extension of the main
Boston - Abbotsbury Macmillan Way

Published by
The Macmillan Way Association,
St Mary's Barn, Pillerton Priors,
Warwick CV35 0PG

© The Macmillan Way Association 2006

ISBN   0 9526851 3 2

First published March 2001
This revised colour edition
published February 2006

Front Cover Photograph:
Bicknoller Combe
(see page 30)

Introducing Macmillan Way West

This 102-mile walking route forms a link between the main (Boston - Abbotsbury) Macmillan Way at Castle Cary and the South-West Coast Path at Barnstaple, with an intermediate link to the northern terminus of the South-West Coast Path at Minehead. Castle Cary is 244 miles from Boston, so it is now possible to walk across England on a fine coast-to-coast route from Boston to Barnstaple - a total distance of no less than 346 miles. Like the Macmillan Way itself, Macmillan Way West has been developed to increase public awareness of Macmillan Cancer Relief and to assist in the raising of further funds for this vitally important charitable organisation, whose role is to improve the lives of people with cancer and their families. In view of this, anyone walking along this path can feel that they are walking 'Across Country for Cancer Care', as our waymark logo proudly proclaims along the whole course of the route. Like most long-distance paths, Macmillan Way West follows existing footpaths, bridleways and byways, and small stretches of minor roads when these are unavoidable.

From Castle Cary, the town where Douglas Macmillan, the founder of Macmillan Cancer Relief, spent his early years, the Way heads westwards across quiet meadowlands. Much of this initial walk closely follows the little River Cary until it goes southwards beyond the delightful town of Somerton soon to start its long journey across the lovely open-sky country of the Somerset Levels, first following beside the River Yeo and then, from Langport, the River Parrett. The Way keeps beside the River Parrett for about six miles, following the course of the Parrett Trail, but after crossing the Bridgwater and Taunton Canal, it heads into the busy little town of North Petherton.

From here the Way immediately starts to climb up on to the beautifully wooded south-eastern flanks of the Quantocks, passing the interesting Fyne Court Visitor Centre before going on to more open country, with the outstanding viewpoint of Cothelstone Hill at its centre. The Way now drops down into the vale to follow along the partly wooded western slopes of the Quantocks before climbing up to follow part of the `spine track' along the tops again. Near the northern end of the Quantocks the Way drops down through the village of Bicknoller and heads across valley country to the bright little town of Williton, just south of the coast at Watchet. The Way now heads west again, across gentle hill country, passing close to historic Cleeve Abbey and through the small village of Withycombe before entering Exmoor National Park.

Climbing steeply into partly wooded, partly bracken-covered country, the Way passes through the ramparts of an Iron Age hill fort, before dropping down to the delightful and deservedly popular village of Dunster. The Way then climbs up steep Grabbist Hill and after a fine ridge walk there is a choice of routes - onwards for those heading for Barnstaple, or down northwards if bustling Minehead is the chosen destination. The main route heads further along the ridge and then plunges down through woods to Wootton Courtenay. From here the serious business of the Exmoor crossing begins and walkers should take note of the advice on page 7.

The Way now leaves the valley and starts the steady climb up to Dunkery Beacon, the highest point on the Macmillan network. From here the Way heads westwards and then south for about fourteen miles across some of Exmoor's wildest and most beautiful country, to arrive at Mole's Chamber - little more than a bend in the road where a miners' inn once stood. From here the Way follows a road for a short way before dropping off the moor and following the Tarka Trail down deep wooded valleys beside clear streams much loved by Tarka's creator, Henry Williamson. Beyond Landkey, the Landkey Brook, another of Tarka's favourites, provides inspiration for the Way's route to the banks of the River Taw, which it follows until reaching Barnstaple's fine 16-arch bridge - the end of its 102-mile journey from Castle Cary - and its second and final link to the South-West Coast Path.

How to Use this Guide

This guide to the 102-mile-long Macmillan Way West is in two parts: The first, an introductory section giving some of the background to its creation and use, the second, a detailed description of the path itself, divided into five chapters, varying in length according to the appropriate stopping and starting points. The Key Map inside the front cover shows the coverage of each chapter while the contents are shown on the Title Page opposite, including the map content of each chapter.

Each of the 24 double-page spreads is entirely self-contained, with map, text and possible illustration all inter-relating. This will ensure that when the book is opened out and inserted into a transparent map case, it can stay there until the next map section is reached. The maps are at a scale of 1:50,000 (about one-and-a-quarter inches to the mile) and are based upon the Ordnance Survey's Landranger series. The sheet numbers of the Ordnance Survey's Landranger and Explorer maps covering the area similar to that covered by each of our own maps are also indicated.

The symbols and signs used on the maps are shown in the block below.

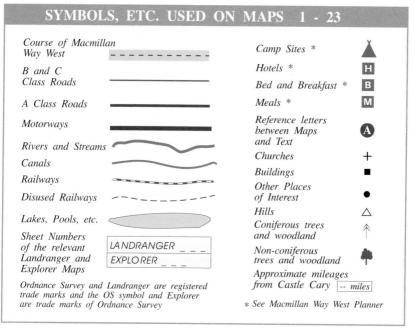

Ordnance Survey and Landranger are registered trade marks and the OS symbol and Explorer are trade marks of Ordnance Survey

* See Macmillan Way West Planner

Each paragraph of text starts with a reference letter and this cross-refers with the same letter on the accompanying map. All information not concerned with the main Macmillan Way West route is shown in italics, while the route details themselves are in normal type. It will also be noted that progressive mileages from Castle Cary are clearly displayed on every map and this will allow users to work out very simply the distance between any two points. It will also enable users to see how far they have gone and, by subtracting from the total of 102, to work out how far they are away from Barnstaple. There is also a mileage chart on page 5.

3

The 24 maps show the location of hotels, bed and breakfasts and meal places, either indicating their presence by being appended to the name of the appropriate town or village, or if well outside any town or village, their exact location. Details of these facilities are constantly changing and are not therefore included in this guide. However, these details will be found in the small frequently up-dated

Barnstaple - our final destination

supplementary leaflet, *The Macmillan Way West Planner*, which is available from the Macmillan Way Association, St Mary's Barn, Pillerton Priors, Warwick CV35 0PG. Please send a stamped and addressed envelope and a cheque *(made payable to the Macmillan Way Association)* for £2.50, all of which will be passed directly to Macmillan Cancer Relief (if you wish to send more it would be gratefully received!).

With the help of information in this guidebook it should be possible to follow Macmillan Way West without further guidance. However, the route from Castle Cary to Barnstaple is also waymarked with Macmillan Way waymarks, apart from sections using public roads and on the open sections of the Quantocks and Exmoor, where they have been kept to an absolute minimum to meet the requirements of these very sensitive areas. The waymarks are of three types - a self-contained plastic roundel with arrow and Macmillan Way logo, a self-adhesive sticker with Macmillan Way logo, which is stuck on a standard yellow or blue waymark arrow (yellow for footpath and blue for bridleway) and (only sporadically) in the Exmoor National Park, wooden signs with the word MAC inscribed. We hope that you have no difficulties, but if any are encountered it would be appreciated if you could let us have the details - *The Macmillan Way Association, St Mary's Barn, Pillerton Priors, Warwick CV35 0PG*. This will help us maintain the existing trail and improve it where necessary.

Walk Macmillan - Support Macmillan

Macmillan Way West and its big-brother, the Macmillan Way have been developed as a tribute to Douglas Macmillan, the founder of the organisation now known as Macmillan Cancer Relief. They are being used by an increasing number of people who have discovered the particular pleasure of walking across country. If you haven't tried it yet - now is the time!

We are also hoping that these pathways will help to raise funds for Macmillan Cancer Relief (see page 6) and with this in mind, might we suggest that you 'sponsor' yourselves for a small sum per mile and ask your friends and relations to help out by also becoming your sponsors. When you have finished your walk we could, should you so wish, let you have a Certificate of Congratulations. If you have managed to collect some sponsorship money (either from yourself, or from your friends and relations), this would of course be gratefully acknowledged on your Certificate.

Do let us have your comments, both on the Pathway itself, and on the way we are organising it. They would be very welcome. Letters to: *The Macmillan Way Association, St Mary's Barn, Pillerton Priors, Warwick CV35 0PG*.

ORDNANCE SURVEY MAP COVERAGE OF MACMILLAN WAY WEST

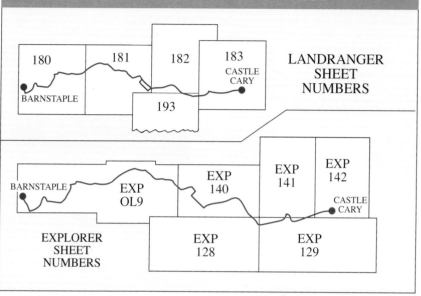

A LIST OF TOWNS AND VILLAGES ON MACMILLAN WAY WEST WITH MILEAGES FROM CASTLE CARY AND BARNSTAPLE

Castle Cary	0	102	Williton	50	52
Keinton Mandeville	6	96	Lower Roadwater	54	48
Charlton Adam	8	94	Withycombe	57	45
Somerton	11	91	Dunster	60	42
Long Sutton	14	88	(Minehead)	65	37
Huish Episcopi	17	85	Wootton Courtenay	64	38
Langport	18	84	Dunkery Beacon	68	34
Oath	21	81	Warren Farm	75	27
Staithe	22	80	Exe Head	78	24
Burrowbridge	23	79	Mole's Chamber	82	20
Moorland	25	77	Whitefield	85	17
Fordgate	27	75	Newtown Bridge	88	14
North Petherton	29	73	West Blakewell	89	13
Broomfield	34	68	East Buckland	90	12
Cothelstone Hill	37	65	West Buckland	92	10
Cothelstone	38	64	Gunn	94	8
West Bagborough	40	62	Swimbridge Newland	97	5
Triscombe	42	60	Landkey	98	4
Bicknoller	47	55	Bishop's Tawton	100	2
Sampford Brett	49	53	Barnstaple	102	0

Macmillan Cancer Relief

The Macmillan Way is dedicated to the memory of Douglas Macmillan, MBE, who founded the organisation now known as Macmillan Cancer Relief in 1911, after the death of his father from cancer. Douglas Macmillan grew up in Castle Cary, where the Macmillan Way West branches off the main Macmillan Way.

Macmillan believed that by improving the knowledge of cancer among the public and health professionals, the needs of people with cancer would be better understood and their quality of life improved. His forward-looking vision still underpins our work today.

Macmillan Cancer Relief supports people who are living with cancer. Every day over 700 people in the UK are told that they have cancer. Our aim is to support people from the moment they first suspect they have cancer, and to ensure that they get the best possible information, treatment and care.

There are now around 2,700 Macmillan nurses, plus over 350 doctors and 250 other health and social care professionals, working in hospitals and in the community. In addition to supporting patients directly, they share their specialist knowledge and skills to help improve standards of treatment and care for everyone with cancer.

As well as taking action today, we're shaping the future of cancer care. Our increasing range of services also includes cancer care centres, a range of cancer information, practical help at home, carer support services, grants and money advice. You can find out more about our services by calling the Macmillan CancerLine on 0808 808 2020.

Helen Lawrey
Macmillan Nurse

We hope that the two Macmillan Ways, which have raised over £250,000 so far, will continue to help raise awareness of Macmillan Cancer Relief, and raise further money to fund our much needed services. One in three people in the UK will be diagnosed with cancer at some time in their life, so directly or indirectly it affects us all.

With your support, Macmillan can change the lives of people living with cancer today -- and tomorrow.

> Macmillan CancerLine 0808 808 2020
> www.macmillan.org.uk .

Safety on Exmoor

On most of the route of Macmillan Way West normal walker's all-weather kit should suffice. However, for the crossing of Exmoor it is essential that walkers can navigate effectively as conditions can change very quickly, even in summer. Do ensure that you have a reserve of food and drink, a whistle, a compass and a copy of the Ordnance Survey's 1: 25,000 Explorer Map No OL9 - Exmoor. The latter indicates all the route between Sampford Brett and Barnstaple and should the weather deteriorate this and the compass will be invaluable aids on the more open sections of Exmoor where the waymarking is less frequent.

A Country Code for Macmillan Way West Walkers

Be safe - **plan ahead** and follow signs. Be prepared for the unexpected. Please respect the working life of the countryside, as our actions can affect people's livelihoods, our heritage, and the safety and welfare of animals and ourselves. Keep to public paths across farmland *and walk in single file to minimise path-spread or crop damage.* Use gates and stiles to cross fences, hedges and walls. **Leave gates and property as you find them**. Take your litter home (*nice thought, but if you are some days away from home, dump it in a litter bin in the next village you pass through*). Don't forget that litter is not only untidy, but it can also cause great harm to animals and farm machinery. Make sure you don't harm animals, birds, plants or trees. **Keep dogs under close control,** *keeping them on leads when there is any chance of encountering stock. Don't forget that pregnant ewes are very much at risk even from merely playful dogs.* It is your duty to ensure that your dog is not a danger or a nuisance to farm animals, wildlife or other people. Take special care on country roads, *usually walk towards oncoming traffic, but on blind bends walk on the outside of the bend where you will be most visible.* Make no unnecessary noise. Show consideration for other people and help to make the countryside a pleasant place for all, at home, at work or at leisure.

A Friendly Countryside for All

While planning the Macmillan Way and Macmillan Way West we have received great kindness from many land owners and tenant farmers and we have assured them that walkers along our path will go quietly through their land and that you will not give offence. If you look at things from country people's point of view, they are far more likely to appreciate yours.

When meeting anyone on your journey, take time to stop and pass the time of day with them. Many farmers and farm workers to whom we have talked, say how surprised they are by the number of walkers who just plod by without even saying hello. Stop to talk and you could well learn so much more about the country through which you are passing. Don't be discouraged if you don't always get a response, but keep trying - the overall result will be well worthwhile, and the next Macmillan Way West walkers that come along are more likely to have a friendly welcome. We have all got to live together, so please - let co-operation be your watchword, rather than confrontation. We are sure that you won't regret it.

Dunkery Beacon - our high point

Our route to Somerton goes across largely flat country, keeping mostly to the valley of the little River Cary. There are no outstanding features of interest, but the very quiet journey provides an ideal introduction to the diverse landscapes that we shall be passing through before reaching Barnstaple, some 102 miles ahead.

Before setting out from Castle Cary do spare time to explore this delightful little market town situated below the earthworks of its early 12th-century castle, with colourful shops, hotels and inns - all full of character. The Victorian Market Hall is now partly a museum displaying farm machinery. Just behind it is the handsome 18th-century stone Post Office and the Round House or Pepper Pot, a stout little circular lock-up built in 1779. The slender-spired church lies some way to the right of our route out of the town and was largely re-built in the same year as the Market Hall - 1855. Douglas Macmillan, the founder of the organisation now known as Macmillan Cancer Relief, was born in Castle Cary in 1884 and grew up here. He spent most of his early years in a house in Upper High Street and walked daily to school in nearby Bruton - a distance of almost three miles each way.

(A) Start from the front of the house in Upper High Street, Castle Cary, where Douglas Macmillan spent his early years and which is marked with a commemorative

The start of our Journey -
Douglas Macmillan lived here

plaque. Go down Upper High Street, soon going straight, not right, into the High Street and joining the main Macmillan Way for a short distance. Pass Market Hall on right and the George Hotel on left. *(The main Macmillan Way turns left just beyond George Hotel, up narrow Paddock Lane on its way south to Abbotsbury.)*

Go straight on along Fore Street. Bear left by war memorial and pond, onto wider road which is Park Street. Just before passing church on right, veer left off Park Street by Castle Cary Primary School onto smaller road (The Park). Go beyond end of surfaced road and onto surfaced path. Through kissing gate into narrow field and through 2nd kissing gate at end of field. Bear right onto surfaced roadway (Park Avenue) and - - - -

(B) Bear right again onto busier road. Cross this road with care, turning right along left-hand pavement. Turn left up Cockhill Elm Lane which becomes grassy near its end. Over stile beside

8

large metal gate and initially keep close to right-hand hedge, but soon veer diagonally left down across field aiming just to left of modern barn in valley. *Good views ahead over flat, pastoral country through which the little River Cary winds.* Soon over double stile at right-hand end of hedgeline and go diagonally left across next field, still aiming to left-hand side of barn. Through gateway and turn right in farmyard and go along track beyond with hedge on both sides. Soon turn left to go over stile and go down field keeping to immediate right of left-

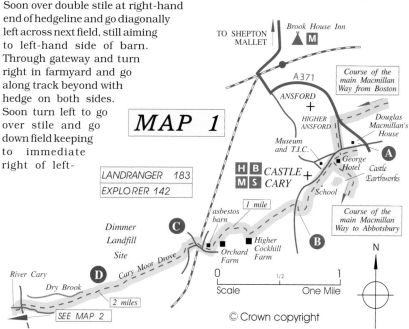

hand hedge. At corner of field bear left over stile beside metal gate and go down short track. Through large metal gate and aim for stile to right of Orchard Farm's buildings. Over stile in fenceline and aim to left of asbestos barn. Veer slightly right beyond barn, go over stile and turn right onto public road. Go straight, not right, at road junction (*no sign*) and over bridge crossing railway line.

(C) Just beyond bridge bear left at road junction (*no sign*) (ignoring FP sign ahead). After 120 yards, where road bears left, go straight ahead onto track (SP - *Cary Moor Drove*). Go down this green road for about half-a-mile. *This is a delightful green road but sadly it is partly spoiled by the many signs of activity at the large landfill site not far to its right. It is also possible that the peace of the otherwise tranquil Cary Valley will be disturbed by the activities of helicopters from the nearby air base at Yeovilton.*

(D) At end of Cary Moor Drove go through large metal gate and then keep in same direction across small field. *(Between here and Map 2 , Point B, the route may be hard to follow - so please go carefully.)* Over stile and keep in same direction across another small field to go through gap in hedge. Now veer slightly left across next field to go through large metal gate. Keep in same direction across next field and over double stile with sleeper bridge in thick hedge . Veer slightly left aiming for initially indistinct, but wide, gap in cross hedge. Through large metal gate in this gap. Go along left-hand edge of field with the little River Cary to immediate left. Lovington Church visible ahead right. Over stile to right of large metal gate and turn left onto minor road to cross small bridge over River Cary (not very apparent here). Immediately beyond bridge, turn right off road and through large metal gate (SP - *Perry's Bridge*). Now follow right-hand edge of field with River Cary to immediate right.

9

(A) Through gap in hedge and continue to keep River Cary to immediate right. Over double stile with sleeper bridge into next field continuing to keep River Cary to immediate right and bear right into far right-hand corner beside River Cary. Over double stile with sleeper bridge to still follow River Cary along next field, but soon bear right in first corner to go over double stile with sleeper bridge. Now go ahead leaving River Cary well to right and following fragmentary line of trees in field. Over stile by large metal gate and sleeper bridge, keep in same direction with hedge on immediate left and at its end aim for oak tree in middle of field. Keep in same direction beyond oak tree, over double stile and keep in same direction. Over double stile with sleeper bridge in cross hedge with Wheatlawn Farm visible over to left. Veer half-right to cross field diagonally to large metal gate. Golf Course visible beyond River Cary to right. Through gate and keep along left-hand edge of field. Over sleeper bridge and two stiles in left-hand corner below trees. Bear slightly right along right-hand edge of narrow field with hedge on immediate right. Over stile in cross-hedge just to left of right-hand corner and along right-hand edge of next field with hedge on immediate right. Pass small, possibly overgrown pond on left and immediately over double stile with sleeper bridge. Along next field with hedge on immediate right and over stile in boggy right-hand corner partly relieved by sleepers. Keep in same direction across next field, aiming just to left of low-voltage power-pole.

(B) Over single stile with sleeper bridge and turn left onto minor public road. Go on minor road up Perry Hill and at entry to Lower Foddington hamlet (*not signed*) turn right just before small building on right onto Hook Lane (SP - *Lydford Lane*). Initially Hook Lane is well surfaced, but it then becomes grassy. Through hunting gate and, keeping in same direction, follow remains of avenue of trees to far end. Through hunting gate, over large wooden bridge and through second hunting gate. Go up field with hedge to immediate left, through third hunting gate and keep in same direction to go through fourth hunting gate. Through fifth hunting gate onto path between hedges.

(C) Turn left at T-junction of tracks onto attractive, tree-shaded Lydford Lane. Turn right at second T-junction of tracks onto Westover Lane (*no sign*) and after almost half-a-mile, go straight, not left at another junction of tracks (*no sign*) keeping on Westover Lane.

(D) Cross the very busy course of the Fosse Way with great care and go onto track opposite known as Babcary Lane, just to left of Fosseway Farm. *The Fosse Way was built by the Romans a few years after their invasion of Britain in AD43 and ran for 182 miles, between Lincoln and Exeter. For much of its course the main Macmillan Way runs parallel with the Fosse Way and if you have come from Boston or Oakham you will have*

Hook Lane, just beyond Lower Foddington

10

already crosssed it twice - at Stow-on-the-Wold and later, near Castle Combe in Wiltshire. Over large brick bridge crossing railway line and after about 300 yards turn left off Babcary Lane (SP - *Common Lane*). **Watch for this with great care**, this turn can easily be missed, especially in high summer. Over stile and keep

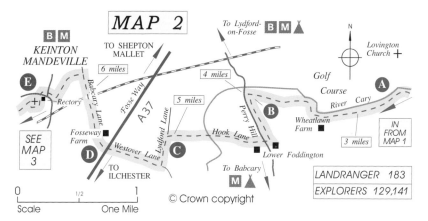

along right-hand edge of field with hedge on immediate right. Over stile beside large metal gate onto grassy track curving left and turn right onto public road into Keinton Mandeville (*no sign*). *Unless visiting one of its inns we go through only the southern end of this extensive stone village, once renowned for the great quarries just to its north. It was also noted for being the birthplace (in 1838) of John Henry Brodribb, the famous Victorian actor who very wisely changed his name to Irving, and who earned instant acclaim for his rendering of 'The Bells'. Although its chancel dates from the 13th century, the church's nave was largely re-built in about 1800 and the building is not of outstanding interest.*

(E) Straight, not right at T-junction by phone box (SP - *Charlton*) into Church Street.Turn left down wide pathway just beyond modern rectory on left and then bear diagonally right across field and enter churchyard through hunting and kissing gates. Circle more than half-way around to left of church to leave churchyard through lych gate. Go across car park and through small gate beside large metal gate. Go across field bearing slightly left to aim for large ash tree. In corner of field go through hunting gate beside stone stile. Kingsweston church spire visible well over to right. Go down field with fragmentary hedge to immediate left.

Keinton Mandeville Church

11

(A) Over stile and turn left to go along left-hand edge of field with hedge to immediate left. In left-hand corner go over stile and turn right into bushy area soon going over sleeper bridge and across field, first aiming for solitary tree and then well to left of buildings of Newcombe Farm. Over stile in hedge to left of Newcombe Farm and turn left to go down track and under railway bridge. Beyond bridge go straight ahead on track known as Withybed Lane and after about 30 yards turn right over stile into field. Go straight across field to opposite hedge. Cross stile beside metal gate into first horse paddock at Pleasant Spot *(not signed)*. Cross this paddock to stile on far side, through gate into second paddock and cross third paddock to stile in far right-hand corner. Initially go along left-hand edge of next field, but where hedge turns left, keep in approximately the same direction across field aiming for middle of

Charlton Adam Church

grey houses. Through double wooden gates and turn right onto public road at entry to Charlton Adam (but turn left if you wish to visit the Fox and Hounds Inn - 15 yards ahead). *There are many pleasant stone houses in the scattered village of Charlton Adam, and its church, dating largely from the 14th century, is worth visiting. There are several good monuments and a Jacobean pulpit.* Turn left at T-junction by Corner Cottage on right (*no sign*). Pass Post Office stores on left and go straight ahead at junction just beyond, passing The Old Chapel on right. Turn right at T-junction overlooked by Vine Cottage and soon bear round to right leaving High Street (*Signed on wall*) and bear left just beyond. Turn right at bottom corner of churchyard and almost immediately turn left to go over stile and straight across field. Through gate and over stile, both below low-voltage power-pole and keep in same direction with fence to immediate left.

(B) Over stile below another power-pole and turn right onto public road with care. Fork left at Y-junction (SP - *Street*) and immediately turn left through large metal gate (SP - *Mill Lane*) to go down driveway track. Pass fine barns and manor house on left and over stile beside large metal gate before turning left onto minor public road. After about 90 yards turn right through stone pillars onto tree-shaded drive-way (SP - *Wellham Road*). After about 130 yards go straight ahead on path with iron railings to right, where driveway

The Cary Valley from Huish Road

swings down left. Through iron kissing gate and keep in same direction through parkland with railings to immediate right. Through 2nd iron kissing gate onto grassy area and pass bungalow on left before bearing right onto public road.

(C) After about 100 yards and just beyond barn on left, turn left to go over stile (SP - *Somerton*). Go diagonally right across large field, towards centre of right-hand facing hedge, to go over footbridge crossing the River Cary. Now bear left and keep up left-hand edge of very large field with hedge on immediate left. At top, left-hand

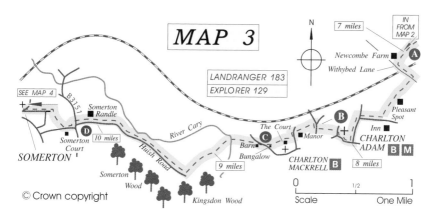

corner, bear left to go through gap before turning right onto rough surfaced lane, which soon becomes a fully surfaced public highway known as Huish Road. Go along Huish Road, with fine woodlands above to left - Somerton Wood. Eventually pass cattle sheds down to right before passing the estate wall of Somerton Randle (house not visible).

(D) Turn left with care onto pavement beside the very busy B3151 and almost immediately **cross road with great care**, to go up minor road to right known as Lower Somerton. Immediately beyond entrance to Granary Lodge and Somerton Court on left, go to right, off road (SP - *Market Square*) up grassy path and over small wooden bridge by house called Downing Brook on right. Over stile into field and up hill keeping to immediate right of fence. Over stile in wooden cross-fence and immediately turn left, now keeping fence to immediate left. Through large metal gate to enter Somerton and keep in same direction down short road. Go slightly right, then left passing Parsonage Close on left and Police Station on right. Arrive at the Market Square, Somerton.

The Market Cross, Somerton

13

Somerton is one of our favourite small market towns, with hotels and inns of character, a wealth of lovely old stone houses and shops, a charming octagonal Market Cross and a fine church. The Market Cross was re-built as late as 1673, but has retained a medieval flavour. The White Hart has fragments of Somerton's castle within its cellars and the old Red Lion has a splendidly dignified 18th-century front. The church has an octagonal tower and its interior is full of interest, including splendid late Perpendicular roofs with angels, an elaborate Jacobean pulpit and several 18th- and early 19th-century monuments.

(A) Go through Market Square, Somerton, with Red Lion Hotel along to right and 17th-century Market Cross and Town Hall to right. Pass Globe Inn and White Hart Inn, both on left and church over to right. Beyond Market Square, keep down West Street, going straight, not left at inverted Y-junction. Pass Unicorn Hotel on right and immediately beyond Hext Almshouses on left and just before railway bridge, turn left down tarmac roadway (SP - *Polhams Lane*). Pass house called Long Orchard on left and now leave Somerton. Just beyond point where roadway bears left away from railway embankment, turn right over stile - do not go through metal gate across track ahead after bend. Go along narrow grassy pathway, still parallel with railway embankment to right and over wooden stile into second small field. Over third stile, pass power-pole on left, over fourth stile into bushy area and immediately turn right through kissing gate. Drop down to minor road and turn left to go along it. Go up minor road with care, now heading towards radio masts. Pass entry to Bedlands Gate Farm on left and Perry Hill Farm on right.

(B) Pass bench on right and turn right at Perry Hill x-rds (*no sign*). Pass Badger's Cross Farm on right and over Badger's Cross x-rds with care (*no sign*). Straight, not right, joining busier road (B3165 - *but not signed here*). Walk with care usually facing oncoming traffic, but always keeping to outside of bends. Soon bear round to left, keeping on B3165, and climb gradual slope.

(C) Near top of hill turn right down surfaced farm road (SP - *Wessex Farm Feeds*). Pass house called Heathlands on right, pass Whitestones bungalow on right, pass pig farm on right. Through wooden gate with bungalow on left and keep straight on at division of tracks by elevated water tank (Sign - *BOCM - Silcock*). Pass portable office on right and keep along left-hand edge of (right-hand) bungalow garden - do not disturb occupiers. Through wooden gate at end of garden and keep in same direction along track with hedge to left and fence to right. Turn left at junction of tracks and into Mundays's Court Lane (possibly going through metal gate) (*no sign*). At end of gradually descending, tree-sheltered section emerge into open section of track *with truly magic views ahead over the head of the Somerset Levels to (from left to right) Montacute, Ham Hill, the distant Blackdown Hills and, one of our destinations, the Quantocks.* Drop down track to go onto surfaced road running between Munday's Court (on left) and Lower Munday (house) on right. Bear round to right on road and almost immediately turn left over stile marked A372 and down field with hedge to immediate right. Over two stiles, one wooden and one stone, and keep in same direction down across parkland, with view of manor house over to left, following line of horse-chestnut trees. Through small wooden gate in bottom right-hand corner of parkland, entering Long Sutton.

(D) Cross busy A372 with great care and go down pavement on left-hand side of Shute Lane into village (SP - *Long Load*) gradually bearing left. *On ground slightly* *higher than the levels we are about to cross, Long Sutton has a pleasant green overlooked by the Devonshire Arms, a fine church and a number of attractive stone houses. Most of the church was built in about 1490 and is well worth visiting. It has a tall west tower, a colourfully restored rood screen, a wagon roof to its chancel and, to its nave, a fine beamed roof with angels.* Pass phone box on left and then turn right at x-rds by the Devonshire

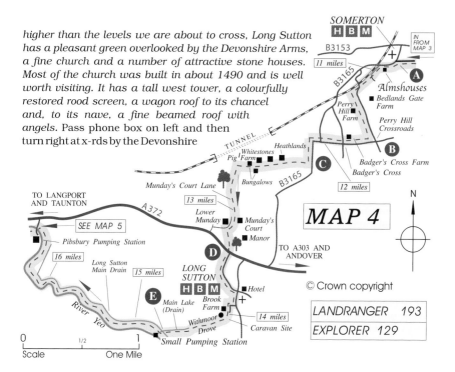

Arms Hotel (SP - *Martock*) to go down right-hand pavement with village green and church over to left. Pass village shop on right and, opposite The Pump House, turn right down New Street. After about 40 yards turn left by New Street House on right and, keeping on surfaced road, pass Brook Farm on right. Pass small caravan site on right and follow lane as it bends to right and becomes known as Withmoor Drove, the surface of which gradually deteriorates. Now heading westwards and entering the Somerset Levels, this part of which is known as Long Load. *Pass sign on right indicating that this is an 'environmentally sensitive area' with bird nesting and feeding grounds - please read carefully.* Through metal hunting gate at end of Withmoor Drove (SP - *River Yeo*) and alongside ditch on right, known as Main Lake. Through metal hunting gate and look back for good view of Long Sutton's church tower.

(E) After a few yards turn right, over stile and bear right to follow the north bank of the River Yeo. Note the drain which will keep on our right almost as far as the Pibsbury Pumping Station, this being known as Long Sutton Main Drain. *For anyone who has walked from Boston, this Somerset Levels section of Macmillan Way West will bring back memories of the fens - it is very similar - partly man-made, but with a very special character (see also page 17).* Through metal hunting gate, the towers of Huish Episcopi and Langport churches visible ahead right. Follow path as it veers slightly away from river to cut across one of its bends. Through metal hunting gate and go below low-voltage power-line. Through metal hunting gate - good view over to left of Muchelney church tower and the abbey beyond it. Through metal hunting gate and now start to bend northwards. Through metal hunting gate and follow meandering River Yeo. Through metal hunting gate, now entering a possibly ungrazed section of river bank. Through metal hunting gate into Pibsbury Pumping Station area, with the station itself on the opposite bank and a large sluice-gate across the river.

15

(A) Turn left onto surfaced roadway to cross bridge over River Yeo (do not attempt to go straight ahead along north bank - it is obstructed further on). At end of bridge turn right over stile beside metal gate (*no sign*) and go along south bank of the River Yeo. Very large meadow to left with Horsey Farm in its centre. Go below low-voltage power-line. Good view of Muchelney church tower well over to left. Where River Yeo bends right, if possible cut across meadow aiming for left-hand end of bridge, thereby keeping as far away as possible from group of buildings on opposite bank of river. Under low-voltage power-line and soon go through metal gate to left of bridge.

(B) Turn right with care onto public road and go over Bicknell's Bridge crossing River Yeo. Turn left off road just beyond Swanston House on left and over stile beside metal gate (SP - *Huish Bridge*). Cross small field diagonally right keeping close to small drainage ditch on left - the Long Sutton Catchwater. Go over stile beside metal gate into more open field with River Yeo a little further over to left, beyond the Long Sutton Catchwater. Go across this field aiming slightly to left of Langport church tower. At end of field, go over metal and stone stile and turn left onto minor road to cross bridge over the Long Sutton Catchwater (but turn right if you wish to visit Huish Episcopi Church (about 600 yards). *Noted for its fine 15th-century west tower and its Norman south doorway, this church also has a window by Burne-Jones.* Beyond this turn right to go to parking area (but for the moment go just beyond to Huish Bridge which overlooks the point where the River Yeo flows into the River Parrett). Now return to parking area. **This is the point where we are joined from the end of the Macmillan Ways' Abbotsbury-Langport Link, coming up from the south beside the River Parrett.** Now leave car parking area going along right bank of River Parrett with fine views of Langport church tower ahead. Ignore wooden bridge on right which appears to mark the end of the Long Sutton Catchwater and ignore second footbridge on right - just visible in bushes. Keep along river bank passing bungalows on right and over footbridge by small sluice and turn right to follow the Parrett Trail into large car park with shops to left and toilets to right. *The Parrett Trail is a 50-mile pathway largely following the course of the River Parrett from its source near Chedington to its outflow into the Bristol Channel well beyond Bridgwater. We shall follow it for some ten miles.* Immediately beyond large car park in Langport, turn left down Bow Street (SP - *Taunton A378)*, soon passing Old Custom House Inn on left and United Reform Church on right.

But turn right if you wish to explore Langport and shop for provisions, keeping in mind that you will not come across any more shops until reaching North Petherton, some 11 miles ahead. This a busy little market town dominated by its handsome, largely Perpendicular church, which has a fine tower providing splendid views over the levels. Just to its east, built over a gateway, is the Hanging Chapel and in the town below there is a wealth of pleasant old buildings including an 18th-century Guildhall.

(C) Turn right opposite newsagent's and go down pathway between houses and walls (SP - *River Parrett Trail*) (*If you wish to visit the Langport and River Parrett Visitor Centre, go straight down A378, cross the River Parrett and turn down left immediately beyond bridge, before returning to this point).* Through kissing gate and veer left across part of large meadow (Northstreet Moor) aiming for gate on raised river bank. Bear right through this large metal gate and resume walking alongside the River Parrett, which is now on immediate left. Under low-voltage power-line. Through kissing gate, under bridge beneath railway line and soon through second kissing gate beside large metal gate to continue along footpath beside river. Through three metal hunting gates. Wooded Aller Hill now lies across to our right.

16

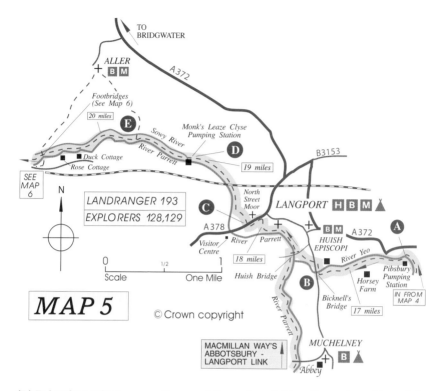

(D) Below low-voltage power-lines and through metal hunting gate and bear left onto broad track by Monk's Leaze Clyse Pumping Station and sluice gate (note interesting explanatory notice-board). Keep on broad track beside river. Note flood relief channel, parallel to right - this is the Sowy River. Long line of the Blackdown Hills becomes visible well over to left when the nearer, wooded hills to left - Hellard's Hill and Red Hill - are passed.

(E) Through metal hunting gate and pass small tree to left and keep as close to river bank as possible. Aller church now visible over to right; take path to right if you wish to visit it - *see note at the top of page 18.* Keep in same direction, temporarily veering away from River Parrett as it bends well to left, go below low-voltage power-line, through metal hunting gate and now re-join river bank. Pass two white-painted cottages over to left, beyond river - Duck Cottage and Rose Cottage - and soon go straight across another river-bend. Through metal hunting gate just before passing house on far bank with brick chimney in garden - this was once part of a withy yard - *see penultimate paragraph on page 18.*

The Somerset Levels are a very extensive area lying for the most part below sea-level. Until well into medieval times they were covered by the sea for much of the year, but some drainage work had been started by the 15th century. However the present network of ditches, or rhines, was constructed between the 17th and 19th centuries. It is an area of great fascination with wonderful bird-watching, its memories of Alfred and the Danes and the defeat of Monmouth; also its island villages, its great pumping stations, its herds of beef and dairy cattle and its long, reed-lined rhines and great withy beds - all lying beneath wide fenland skies.

The village of Aller is best reached from Point E on Map 5, although a return may be made to Point A on this map. The interesting little church here was the scene of a remarkable ceremony in the year 879. King Alfred had finally defeated Guthrum, King of the Danes, at nearby Athelney and as part of their peace terms, Guthrum and 30 of his men agreed to be baptised into the Christian Church.

(A) Pass substantial metal footbridge over river to left, but do not cross it. Beyond footbridge keep on path on right of River Parrett, with views of little hill well ahead - Burrow Mump. Oath Farm now visible across river to left. Over stile beside metal gate and Oath Lock visible ahead left - this is a sluice-gate at the head of the tidal section of the River Parrett. *Before the building of Oath Lock the River Parrett was tidal as far as Langport.* Cut across another bend in the river - this one filled in by an excavated pool, which is usually occupied by a number of swans. *Look back left to see the Burton Pynsent Monument on wooded ridge, a tall Tuscan column rising above the trees. This was erected by Capability Brown in 1765, the same year that Sir William Pynsent left the mansion of Burton Pynsent to William Pitt 'as a token of his enthusiastic esteem'.*

Oath Lock - The Parrett is tidal below here.

Through metal hunting gate with line of trees to right. Pass brick-built West Sedgemoor Pumping Station over to left beyond the Parrett - this large station controls the drainage of the whole of West Sedge Moor - an area stretching about four miles to the south and west of here. Now starting to pass the scattered hamlet of Stathe to left beyond the Parrett.

(B) Over stile in wooden fence and after a few yards go straight ahead on track to go through gate (SP - Parrett Trail) *(But go left, over bridge if you wish to look at willow sculptures in withy yard to left - private property. Withy yards are places where withies are boiled in bundles to make them more pliable prior to their being woven into baskets, hampers, fish traps and other containers.)* Keep along track following course of River Parrett, still on left. Burrow Mump (see below) looms ahead;

Burrow Mump and the River Parett

18

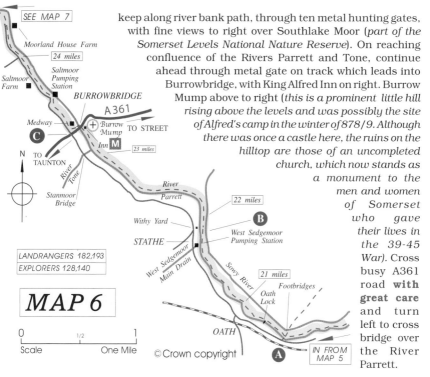

SEE MAP 7

Moorland House Farm

24 miles

Saltmoor Pumping Station

Saltmoor Farm

BURROWBRIDGE

A361

Medway

Burrow Mump · TO STREET

C

Inn **M**

23 miles

N

TO TAUNTON

River Tone

Stanmoor Bridge

River Parrett

22 miles

B

Withy Yard

West Sedgemoor Pumping Station

STATHE

West Sedgemoor Main Drain

Sowy River

21 miles

Footbridges

Oath Lock

LANDRANGERS 182,193

EXPLORERS 128,140

MAP 6

0   1/2   1

Scale   One Mile

©Crown copyright

OATH

A

IN FROM MAP 5

keep along river bank path, through ten metal hunting gates, with fine views to right over Southlake Moor (*part of the Somerset Levels National Nature Reserve*). On reaching confluence of the Rivers Parrett and Tone, continue ahead through metal gate on track which leads into Burrowbridge, with King Alfred Inn on right. Burrow Mump above to right (*this is a prominent little hill rising above the levels and was possibly the site of Alfred's camp in the winter of 878/9. Although there was once a castle here, the ruins on the hilltop are those of an uncompleted church, which now stands as a monument to the men and women of Somerset who gave their lives in the 39-45 War*). Cross busy A361 road **with great care** and turn left to cross bridge over the River Parrett.

(C) Soon turn right at small x-rds (SP -*Moorland*). Pass entrance to house called Medway on right and keep along road with care. Pass village hall on right and houses on right, not far beyond. Follow road as it bends round to right and then bends to left by small Saltmoor Pumping Station on right. River Parrett now alongside on right again. Do **not** try to go up onto bank a few yards beyond but keep on road. Observe direction of water in river as, being tidal, it could be flowing either way. Lovibonds Farm beyond opposite bank, to right. Pass Saltmoor Cottage on left and Saltmoor Farm just beyond, also on left. Pass Myrtle Tree Farm on left. Pass handsome, mellow-brick Manor Farmhouse on left.

Straight, not left, going onto no-through road (*no sign*). Pass Heronsgate (house), Hale's Farm and Millwood Farm - all on left. Pass

Inquisitive cattle beside the River Parett near Moorland

Moorland House Farm, on right beyond the river. Arrive at end of road and through gap beside large metal gate onto surfaced track, still beside the River Parrett, with Coates Farm down to left.

19

(A) Pass pleasant mellow-brick cottage over to right, just beyond river. Go around left-hand bend with good view of the Quantocks ahead. Pass derelict cottage on left. *Westonzoyland's fine church tower visible well over to right. This lies just to the south of the site of the Battle of Sedgemoor, where on 6th July 1685, the rabble led by the Duke of Monmouth suffered total defeat at the hands of Colonel Kirke's disciplined troops.* Go straight through metal gate keeping on river bank by Riverside Cottage at entry to Moorland hamlet on left - no shop, no inn. Over small stile and keep along river bank. Westonzoyland Pumping Station with brick chimney now visible ahead. Through elegant, inverted-ogival squeeze-stile and soon pass pumping station across river to right. Over stile with interesting noticeboard providing information on the Westonzoyland Pumping Station, the first to be built in the Somerset

The River Parrett near Moorland

Levels (1830). *The great steam engine and scoop-wheel, which were installed in 1862, are no longer in use but the station is now run as a lively museum project by the Westonzoyland Engines Trust. Unfortunately there is no way across from our path on the opposite bank.* Over stile beyond sharp bend to left.

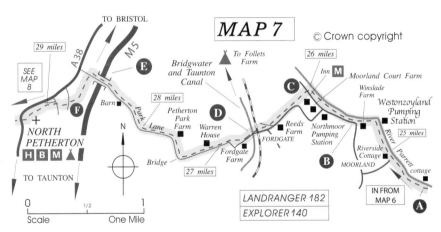

(B) Over wooden stile just beyond Winslade Farm to left and continue along road just below to its left. Straight, not left, beyond farm with stable buildings, joining busier road at junction (SP - *Huntworth*). Go down narrow and quite busy road, but if possible go up onto bank above to right to walk parallel to road. Pass Laburnum Cottage on left. Pass phone box on left immediately before Northmoor Pumping Station, also on left. Straight, not left at road junction (*no sign*) and soon pass Moorland Court Farm on left.

(C) Pass Thatchers Arms on left and within 30 yards turn left immediately beyond small terrace of houses, down small path. Over stile at end of bushy area and keep in same direction down field to immediate left of open drain. Over wooden railings with step and immediately over stile to right of bungalow. Down narrow pathway between wall on left and hedge on right and soon over stile. Continue in same direction along public road, still with drain to immediate right. Enter Fordgate hamlet and fork left by Reeds Farm on left and go up slope. Bear right at road junction (*no sign*) and immediately cross bridge over railway line. At miniature x-rds go straight ahead on tarmac roadway.

(D) Over swing-bridge crossing the Bridgwater and Taunton Canal and keep straight up farm track (SP - *Fordgate Farm - Private*). Here we leave the course of the Parrett Trail, which heads northwards along the canal towpath. *The Bridgwater and Taunton Canal, part of a grandiose project to link Bristol with the Grand Western Canal between Taunton and Exeter, was completed in 1841. It was soon overtaken by the coming of the railways and has been re-opened only in 1994.* Just before Fordgate Farm's buildings on left, fork right to follow waymarked path across field. After about 250 yards join farm track and keep in same direction. *The Quantocks visible ahead, but they do not look very dramatic from here, less so than the dark outline of the Blackdown Hills, visible well over to left.* Pass Warren House on right and after 250 yards follow track as it bends sharply to right and crosses bridge over sunken watercourse. Keep on track to left of extensive farm buildings and farmhouse of Petherton Park Farm and farm cottages just beyond. Now on Park Lane where noise from M5 motorway becomes apparent. Over cattle-grid, up slightly better surfaced roadway and under two high-voltage power-lines. Bear round to right on entering orchard area and after about 500 yards pass barn on left with two water tanks on stands just beyond.

(E) After about 400 yards cross bridge over the M5 motorway and after about 200 yards turn left over stile. Follow path with hedge to immediate left. Over stile at end of field, cross tarmac roadway and small parking area and go through kissing gate to cross right-hand edge of children's play area with tennis courts. Keep in same direction, going through gap in hedge and along right-hand edge of sports field.

(F) Turn right through kissing gate and turn sharp right to go along narrow pathway with laplink fencing on both sides and enter outskirts of North Petherton. Turn left onto road in housing estate and soon turn right into Sunnybrow Close. Now heading directly towards church tower. At end of close go down narrow pathway and then turn right onto narrow road. Soon go left up further pathway with stone retaining walls on either side. Pathway soon widens into roadway with houses on both sides. Bear right just beyond end of roadway in Ellen Close and then bear left with care opposite the Lamb Inn onto pavement beside the still busy A38. Pass several useful shops on left and the Walnut Tree Hotel on right before arriving at the fine Parish Church, which is at the centre of North Petherton.

The Bridgwater and Taunton Canal, near our crossing point

The A38 through North Petherton is still over-busy with traffic despite the M5 motorway running close by. However this small town has several useful shops, which should be used by those heading over the Quantocks, where supplies are impossible to find. The largely late 15th-century church has a splendid tower in the best Somerset tradition, with elaborately traceried bell openings. Its interior has been sympathetically restored and in its well-mown churchyard is a fine cross, contemporary with the church.

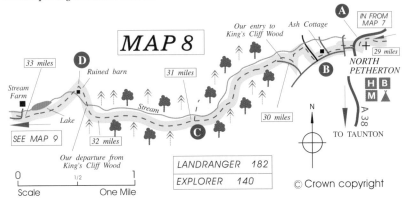

MAP 8

(A) Pass North Petherton Parish Church on left and bear round to left, keeping on A38 and passing Community Centre and toilets just beyond, both on left. Pass phone box on right and turn right **with great care**, off A38 to go up Tappers Lane by the West End Bakery (*no sign*). Keep straight up Tappers Lane and then go over offset x-rds, up Cliff Road (SP - *Clavelshay*). Keep straight up gradually narrowing Cliff Road, veering slightly left by thatched Ash Cottage with pheasant on its ridge-top.

(B) Turn right at road junction just beyond last house on right (*no sign*) and down even narrower road. In bottom of valley turn left off road just before small bridge to go over stile (SP - *Public footpath*). Go along bottom, right-hand edge of field with fence to immediate right and stream just beyond. *(We shall follow reasonably close to this stream for four miles, almost as far as Broomfield (see page 24). Unfortunately it does not appear to have a name.)* Bear left at end of ever-narrowing field and soon turn right to go over stile in next corner. Turn left to go up left-hand edge of field and over stile in top, left-hand end of field and turn right onto public road. Woodlands now up to left and after 200 yards fork left to go over small parking area at the entry to the extensive King's Cliff Wood. *These woods must owe their origin to their lying within the bounds of the ancient Forest of Petherton, a once*

North Petherton Church

22

Stream beyond King's Cliff Wood

jealously guarded hunting preserve. From this point onwards it may be possible to spot ravens and buzzards, both of which are reasonably common on the Quantocks. **We are now in the Quantock Hills Area of Outstanding Natural Beauty and from here until leaving it near Bicknoller (page 31) we have been asked to use less colourful waymarks, and to use them sparingly, and not at all on the open tops.** Keep up track in beautifully shaded woodlands going straight, not left, at first track junction. We shall start very gradually climbing up into the Quantocks within these woods. Fork right at next track junction, still keeping within lower, right-hand edge of woodlands. Through gap beside stile in short length of cross-fence. Enter a more open area going along a wider track and pass many foxgloves on its edge. Stream visible down to the right.

(C) Bear right onto better surfaced track and ignore footpath dropping down to valley on right (*unless you wish to look at small bridge over cooling stream - less than 100 yards off our route*). Bear left at next Y-junction, keeping on upper track. Bear left at next junction keeping on upper track with stream to right. Continue along same track through dense woodland for about three-quarters-of-a-mile. Track becomes narrower, and maybe boggy in places. Eventually, where track bears round to right at edge of woodlands, bear right at Y-junction. Cross stile and soon go along a boardwalk bridge over stream. Continue with stream to left and woods to right. After 200 yards cross possibly boggy area and keep straight on with small stream still to left.

(D) Turn left at cross-hedge at top right-hand corner of field, follow hedge, now on right, and pass ruined barn on left. Take rubble-covered track across culvert over stream and continue up hill to reach metal gate with stile to left. Cross stile and continue on well defined track for nearly half a mile. Pool visible in valley ahead right. Through metal gate and Stream Farm is almost opposite on right-hand slope of valley. Over stile beside large metal gate and go straight ahead on surfaced public road, passing barns just below to right and still running parallel to stream down below to right.

Pool in valley near Stream Farm

(A) Turn sharp right with care at road junction in woods (*no sign*) and go over small bridge crossing 'our' stream. Pass house up to left called Woodney with large garden. Just beyond garden go up steps to left, leaving road and over stile. Go straight ahead along bottom left-hand side of field with Woodney's boundary fence to immediate left and over stile in bottom corner of field. Immediately turn left over second stile and then turn right to continue in same general direction with fence now to immediate right. Turn left in first corner of field, down short length of fence and then veer diagonally left down towards stile in valley. House with park-like garden and pool on our right. Over modest stile into garden area and over small concrete bridge keeping to bottom edge of garden and aiming for stile ahead on edge of woodlands. Please go quietly and do not linger here. Over a second small concrete bridge on edge of mown area. Leave garden area and over stile into woods. Follow meandering, but well-used path (muddy after rain) through woods with our stream not far to left. Now starting to climb gradually in wood. Turn right by track which has just forded stream to our left *(to join the Quantock Greenway, which we shall follow as far as Ivyton Farm, page 25, para C))* and start to climb more steeply and veer away from our stream - this is the last we shall see of an old friend which has kept us company since North Petherton. At end of woods go straight ahead with care onto minor public road, still going upwards. Where road levels out Broomfield Church is visible ahead right if foliage is not too thick. Definite view of church through gateway to right. Turn sharp right, keeping on public road and church tower now visible straight ahead. Veer round to left by church on right keeping on road. *The unspoilt interior of Broomfield Church has arcade capitals with leaf carvings, fine medieval benches and bench-ends, old stone floors and a 15th-century headless brass in its tower floor.* Pass green overlooked by house with flower-filled garden. Pass entry to Fyne Court Visitor Centre on right. *Do not miss a visit to its most interesting Interpretation Room relating to the Quantocks, as this will make your journey across this outstandingly beautiful hill country even more worthwhile.* **For a brief description of the Quantocks, see page 31.**

(B) Bear right at T-junction (SP - *Bishop's Lydeard*) and pass cottage on right. Almost immediately fork left keeping on wider road and turn left just before phone box on left to go down sunken trackway well to left of metal gate. Go gently down this delightful trackway overhung with trees - it could be rather wet after heavy rain. After about 400 yards fork right keeping on higher of two trackways. *Good views through trees of the Blackdown Hills well over to left.* After 250 yards emerge onto wider track and continue dropping down before crossing small stone bridge beside ford. Now start to climb up track and turn right onto

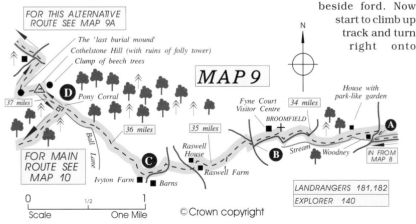

FOR THIS ALTERNATIVE ROUTE SEE MAP 9A

N

The 'last burial mound'
Cothelstone Hill (with ruins of folly tower)
Clump of beech trees

MAP 9

House with park-like garden

37 miles

D Pony Corral

Fyne Court Visitor Centre

34 miles

BROOMFIELD

A

36 miles

35 miles

Ball Lane

Raswell House

C

B Stream Woodney

IN FROM MAP 8

FOR MAIN ROUTE SEE MAP 10

Ivyton Farm

Barns

Raswell Farm

LANDRANGERS 181,182
EXPLORER 140

0   1/2   1
Scale   One Mile

© Crown copyright

24

public road by Raswell House on right and Raswell Farm on left. After about 10 yards turn left off road and go steeply up sunken trackway. At top of trackway go straight ahead onto minor public road.

(C) Go gently down track and then turn right over stile beside large metal gate opposite second barn of Ivyton Farm *(leaving the Quantock Greenway)*. Go up track across field gently curving to left. *On a clear day, distant views over to left of Dorset Hills and long line of Blackdown Hills, with Wellington Monument at their far, western end.* Through metal gate at end of track and immediately turn right over stile beside second gate. Follow up short, right-hand edge of field with hedge on immediate right. Through large metal gate and go diagonally left aiming for stile in cross-hedge. Go over stile and keep in same direction across next field, eventually aiming for gap in left-hand hedge-line. Through gap in hedge and keep in same direction across next field aiming for stile in hedge with scrubby woodlands beyond. Over stile keeping in roughly the same direction across scrubby woodland for about 40 yards to emerge into slightly more open area. At cross-path, turn left, uphill for about 200 yards to stile. Cross stile to emerge onto Ball Lane (trackway). Keep in same direction, going up Ball Lane at this point where it has turned left (westwards). Keep up Ball Lane, keeping to immediate right of hedge-bank, and after about 400 yards go straight, not right at Y-junction.

(D) After another 100 yards, at end of woodlands, turn right through hunting gate initially obscured by tree. Post and rail fences to left are part of a corral used for the control of ponies. Initially go straight ahead across grassy sward with bushes and bracken on both sides. Then bear right by young oak tree on right and follow well-used path, eventually bearing round to right, still climbing gently all the way. The clump of beech trees to right is well to right of the true summit of Cothelstone Hill. Narrow path becomes a broad grassy track as it heads past another clump of trees towards the summit of Cothelstone Hill. *This is marked by the battered remains of an 18th-century folly tower (demolished some years ago) on a mound formed by a Bronze Age round barrow. Cothelstone Hill is possibly the finest of all Quantock viewpoints and encompasses, amongst many other features, Brent Knoll, the Parrett Estuary and Bridgwater Bay, complete with with Flat Holm and Steep Holm. Also Minehead with the sea to its right and North Hill rising behind it, the Brendon Hills and the distant outlines of Exmoor beyond.*

To take the Main Route, turn about at the summit of Cothelstone Hill and re-trace your route towards the hunting gate **(D)** by the pony corral - see below for details. *(But if you wish to take the* **'High-Level Route'** *from Cothelstone Hill turn to page 26 and use Map 9A.)* **For the Main Route** return south-eastwards from Cothelstone Hill, down wide grassy, track keeping well to the right of the clump of beech trees. Soon fork right at junction of tracks and then go back through the hunting gate by the pony corral.

(D) Turn round to right to go between post and rail fences and turn to top of page 28, Point **(A)** which is common with Point **(D)** on this map.

Ponies on Cothelstone Hill

Alternative (High-Level) Route
Cothelstone Hill - top of Triscombe Combe   3 miles

(A) From the summit of Cothelstone Hill head west-south-westwards towards bench hewn out of part of a tree trunk, but take left-hand of two grassy tracks passing to left of bench and also to left of low burial mound. At the last burial mound, astride our track, turn right off grassy track to follow narrower grassy pathway through bracken, gradually losing height. Go below young oak trees and follow path as it leads gently downhill. Go through kissing gate in pony fence and veer right onto well-defined track. Where main track bears down to left, fork right onto pathway through woodlands. Where there is a house visible through trees to left keep straight over x-rds of tracks and then follow path as it veers to right.

(B) Turn left with care onto possibly busy public road and after about 50 yards turn right at road junction by Park End Lodge on left (SP- *Bagborough*). Almost immediately veer left at next road junction. **Walk along this road with care.** Keep along wide right-hand verge of road for half-a-mile as it climbs steadily before going straight, not left, at next road junction (SP - *Lydeard Hill Car Park*). Turn half-right through large wooden gate at first bend on this narrow road to follow pleasant permissive bridleway largely below fine beech trees. Through hunting gate and turn right into Lydeard Hill Car Park. Through gate and go onto lower (left-hand) of two paths *(Sheep grazing here - Dogs must be kept under control). Fine views over to left towards the Brendon Hills and Exmoor.* Continue along level, well-surfaced path, with fenced, park-like field below to left and Lydeard Hill up over brow to right. Now bear right keeping on path and drop down a little.

(C) Over stile to right of large wooden gate with woods now to left. Good view down wooded Aisholt Combe to right, with Middle Hill above to its left. Now starting to climb gradually with good views over the eastern slopes of the Quantocks, with the ground falling away quite steeply to the right of our path. At Y-junction go straight ahead up track (SP - *Public Footpath - No Bikes or Vehicles*). Follow path as it initially bends to left and then bears gently up to right as the gradual ascent of Will's Neck continues. Keep to broad track and summit trig point comes into view.

(D) Arrive at Will's Neck, at 1260ft above sea level, the highest point on the Quantocks. *The views from here take in almost all the features visible from Cothelstone Hill (see page 25) but, in our opinion, this summit is not quite as satisfying as Cothelstone.* Keep to track which passes just to left of trig point and after about 100 yards bear round to right onto smaller track and after another 100 yards turn right onto wider track to go due northwards down hill, with Hinkley Point Power Station visible in the distance straight ahead. Soon veer to left with fine views north-westwards of the western scarp face of

View eastwards from Cothelstone Hill

26

the Quantocks above Triscombe and Crowcombe, with the sea in the distance beyond. Join wider track coming in from right (part of the main 'spine track' - see page 31) and keep straight across wide grassy trackless area. Fence over to left has **Danger** signs upon it as it marks the edge of the great Triscombe Quarry - now no longer in use. Track now becomes better defined, this being part of the spine track, and soon drops down on it into 'valley' taking right-hand fork to arrive at pleasant grassy area with bench beneath hawthorn tree on left.

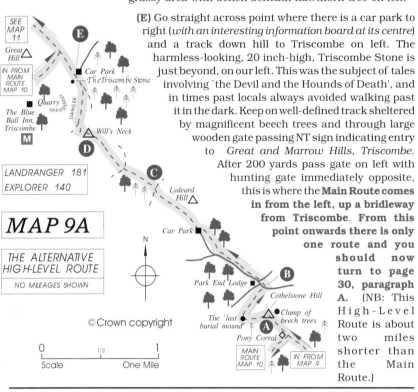

SEE MAP 11

E

Great Hill △

IN FROM MAIN ROUTE MAP 10

Quarry

Car Park The Triscombe Stone

DANGER

The Blue Ball Inn, Triscombe M

Will's Neck △

D

LANDRANGER 181
EXPLORER 140

C

Lydeard Hill △

MAP 9A

THE ALTERNATIVE HIGH-LEVEL ROUTE

NO MILEAGES SHOWN

Car Park ■

N

0   1/2   1
Scale   One Mile

Park End Lodge ■

B

Cothelstone Hill

Clump of beech trees △

The 'last burial mound' ●

A

Pony Corral ◇

MAIN ROUTE MAP 10

IN FROM MAP 9

(E) Go straight across point where there is a car park to right (*with an interesting information board at its centre*) and a track down hill to Triscombe on left. The harmless-looking, 20 inch-high, Triscombe Stone is just beyond, on our left. This was the subject of tales involving `the Devil and the Hounds of Death', and in times past locals always avoided walking past it in the dark. Keep on well-defined track sheltered by magnificent beech trees and through large wooden gate passing NT sign indicating entry to *Great and Marrow Hills, Triscombe*. After 200 yards pass gate on left with hunting gate immediately opposite, this is where the **Main Route comes in from the left, up a bridleway from Triscombe. From this point onwards there is only one route and you should now turn to page 30, paragraph A.** (NB: This High-Level Route is about two miles shorter than the Main Route.)

Cothelstone (see page 28) - *This delightful group of buildings consists of a church, a farm, a few cottages and an exquisite Elizabethan manor house. It was from the manor's gatehouse that three of the Duke of Monmouth's supporters were hanged after his defeat at the Battle of Sedgemoor in 1685. The largely Perpendicular church has a Jacobean pulpit and a good set of 16th-century bench-ends in addition to several interesting monuments to members of the Stawell family, the owners of the manor. The early 19th-century mansion of Cothelstone House, near Terhill, well to the north-west of the manor, was demolished in the 1950's but its fine park, part of which we walk through, is now being gradually brought back to life.*

West Bagborough (see page 28) *Pleasant village with a hotel, an inn and a B&B. At the far end of the village there is an elegant Georgian house just above the church. The interior of the latter was enriched in the 1920s by Sir Ninian Comper, who was responsible for the rood screen, font cover and stained glass. See also the medieval bench-ends and the beautifully carved figures in the porch.*

Triscombe (see page 29) - *Minute hamlet with a colourful little inn, The Blue Ball, and a delightful combe leading up onto the Quantock ridge.*

(A) *(This is common with Point D on page 25)* Turn round to right to go between post and rail fences and through gap into Cothelstone Woods. Now bear well to left and go 25 paces before turning right onto path which soon drops down into extensive woodlands. For a short distance keep parallel with slightly sunken trackway just to right. Join slightly more used bridleway coming in from right. Cross line of other track, with barrier gates on either side of our track. Our track now fairly narrow and probably quite muddy after rain. Now just within the south-eastern edge of the wood, with remains of old quarries amongst trees on right. Follow path as it first turns right and then left, with barrier gate on right. Through hunting gate beside large wooden gate and emerge onto quite busy public road. Keep in same direction, going straight ahead down public road and after 150 yards, just before entering Cothelstone, ignore stile to right. Go through the hamlet of Cothelstone, passing the gateway to Cothelstone Manor on right, with good views of the manor and the church beyond it *(see bottom of page 27)*.

(B) Just beyond these gates, turn right, over metal fence in wall by postbox in wall *(re-joining Quantock Greenway)* and head across field keeping parallel with the manor's driveway. At end of field go through gate and veer slightly right (SP - *Path to Church*) to go in front of house at left side of Court *(be as quiet as possible please)*. Keep on concrete path beyond house and veer round to right. Turn left through wooden gate onto well-defined path across field (but go through to right if you wish to visit interesting church). This field is the start of the partially restored Cothelstone Park *(see bottom of page 27)*, with its mansion once standing in trees ahead right. Note the large lake, possibly just visible over to left. Initially keep in same direction, aiming just to right of poplar trees. In valley veer slightly left, uphill, to go between oak trees ahead until reaching metal farm gate. Through metal gate and along short stretch of track through belt of woodland. Go straight across minor public road with care and up slope to go through gap into field. Go diagonally right, across usually cropped field and at its end go over a wooden stile keeping between fences and up short length of sunken trackway. Go over stile and go straight ahead up minor public road (this is just beyond Terhill hamlet). Go up road quite steeply passing Pilgrim's Cottage on left and after about 100 yards turn left onto permissive bridleway - a reasonably surfaced terrace track with fine views over rolling country to left with the Brendon Hills beyond.

(C) At end of track, turn right onto road at entry to West Bagborough *(see bottom of page 27)* and soon turn left at T-junction by Higher House Hotel. Pass Bashford's Farmhouse and the Rising Sun Inn, both on right.

(D) Pass War Memorial on right and then turn right to go through attractive lych gate. Go up long path towards church, which is situated beside Bagborough House. Go through metal gate into churchyard and turn **very sharp left** to go along lower, left-hand edge of churchyard. At end of churchyard go through wooden gate at its lower, left-hand corner and along terrace pathway between hedges, with parkland down to left and two welcome benches. Cross boggy area at end of terrace and through kissing gate. Go along right-hand edge of field

Cothelstone Manor and Church

28

keeping in same direction and towards end of field join track and keep to immediate right of barn. Go through small wooden gate beside large metal gate and turn right to go through second small wooden gate beside large metal gate. Bear left across next field aiming for wooden gate beside large metal gate. Through this small wooden gate and veer slightly right to go to top right-hand corner of field. Through small wooden gate beside large metal one and across very narrow field to go through metal gate. *Good views back left to the Wellington Monument on top of the distant Blackdowns.* After about 50 paces veer left off track and cross remainder of field to go over stile beside metal gate. Cross a further very narrow field to go through small wooden gate. Now veer slightly right passing Rock Farm's thatched cottage over to right and head for kissing gate in right-hand corner of field.

(E) Through kissing gate and turn right, up initially surfaced roadway passing Rock Farm on right before going ahead increasingly steeply on rougher and narrower track. Through large wooden gate, take left footpath *(marked yellow)*, not bridleway *(marked blue)*. Keep within left-hand edge of woodland, initially climbing steeply and soon forking left to drop down a little. Follow this pleasant path passing cottage visible up to right just before fording a small stream. Straight, not right, joining wider track at inverted Y-junction.

(F) Bear right onto surfaced public road at inverted Y-junction and turn left at T-junction in Triscombe by the back of the Blue Ball Inn *(no sign)*. Pass the Blue Ball Inn, Triscombe on left (but DO NOT turn sharp right to follow Quantock Greenway (South) and almost immediately turn right at road junction opposite thatched building to follow Greenway (North) *(SP - Quantock Greenway)*. After 60 yards, turn right again at T-junction by barn (SP - *Bridleway*) and start climbing steeply on track passing wooden shed on right and soon through large wooden gate entering Great and Marrow Hills NT Area. After 20 paces, go straight up track, ignoring steep path up to left *(where Quantock Greenway (North) leaves our route)*, soon emerging into the attractive open country of Triscombe Combe with bracken-covered slopes up to right and fine beech woods on left. Pass large manhole cover in fenced enclosure to left and after about 200 yards fork right on main track, which continues to bear right. Soon, bear round to left, ignoring a track appearing to continue straight on. Emerging into open moorland, aim for line of beech trees on hill summit. Go through large wooden gate in earth bank and turn left onto tree-sheltered spine track **merging with Alternative (High-Level) Route** *(see page 30, paragraph A).*

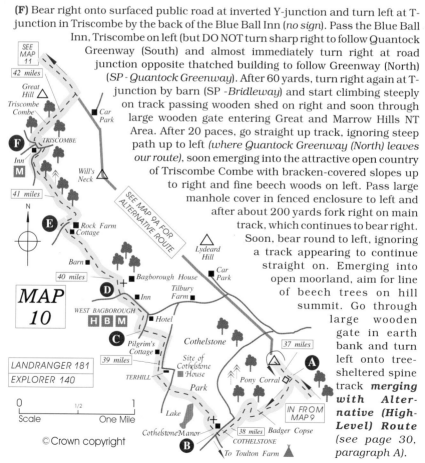

SEE MAP 11
42 miles
Great Hill △
Triscombe Combe
TRISCOMBE
F
Inn
M
Will's Neck △
Car Park
41 miles
N
E ■ Rock Farm ■ Cottage
SEE MAP 9A FOR ALTERNATIVE ROUTE
Lydeard Hill △
Barn ■
40 miles
Bagborough House ■
Car Park
Tilbury Farm ■
MAP 10
D ■ Inn
WEST BAGBOROUGH
H B M ■ Hotel
C Pilgrim's Cottage ■
Cothelstone
37 miles
39 miles
Site of Cothelstone ■ House
TERHILL
A
Pony Corral
Park
LANDRANGER 181
EXPLORER 140
0   1/2   1
Scale   One Mile
© Crown copyright
Lake
Cothelstone Manor
B
38 miles   Badger Copse
COTHELSTONE
To Toulton Farm
IN FROM MAP 9

(A) Having turned left onto the spine track above Triscombe Combe and having been joined by the Alternative (High Level) Route, keep on spine track and after a further 350 yards pass large wooden gate on left. Keep on track through delightful beech wood. Pass gate on left with small pond just beyond it. Through large wooden gate leaving National Trust's Great and Marrow Hills Area and keep on track veering slightly right.

(B) After about 400 yards cross possibly busy public road **with care** with Crowcombe **Combe** Gate just to left (but not apparent) and keep in same direction on track which veers to left after 300 yards by Crowcombe **Park** Gate (Do not go straight ahead up hill). After 150 yards ignore gate and stile to left with footpath sign and keep on track, now gradually starting to rise and veer right, away from trees to left. Pyramid-like Hurley Beacon visible ahead left with good views opening out to left. Keep on track passing stile on left leading to Hurley Beacon and now start to drop down.

(C) Arrive at Halsway Post - now merely a post supporting a number of fire beaters, but a significant meeting point of several tracks. Keep in same (north-westerly) direction to climb gently on wide grassy track, the spine track keeping parallel just to right. Join spine track for a few yards near the brow where grassy path becomes a track. Now drop down a few paces to right and re-join the pronounced spine track. Good views to right down Slaughterhouse Combe, spoilt only by the dreaded Hinkley Point Power Station! Be sure to keep on track, first veering right and then left, around a spur from Thorncombe Hill (above us, to left).

(D) Well before arriving at large open, grassy space with a few scrubby trees visible ahead, **watch with care** for a small triangular stone to left of main track. Here, bear left leaving stone to right. After about 100 yards cross straight over track coming down from Thorncombe Hill, which is to left. Keep on minor track, soon starting to drop down into the head of delightful bracken-covered Bicknoller Combe. The descent here is reasonably gradual and the track/path surface reasonable. Over very small tree-shaded ford; stream, now to our right, becomes more apparent. Just beyond old quarry workings to right, go straight, not right, keeping on track (path to right goes to Weacombe). After about 120 yards go through large wooden

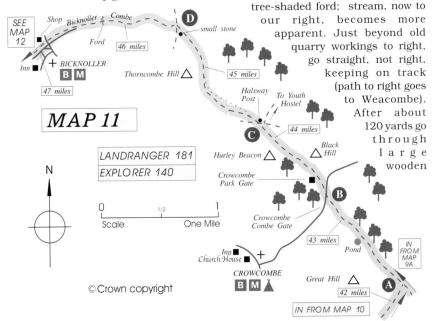

gate leaving National Trust's Bicknoller Hill Area. Now continue down surfaced public road and after about 300 yards enter Bicknoller village. *Church and cottages make a pleasant group near the village centre and cannot have changed much since the poet Coleridge and his friends used to walk over the Quantock ridge from his home at Nether Stowey to take refreshment at Bicknoller's inn. Happily the inn is still here and there is also a lively shop run by the villagers. There is an old cross in the churchyard and the village stocks are close by. The handsome, largely Perpendicular church has a beautiful rood screen and a set of carved medieval bench-ends. 15th-century carvings on the nave capitals and elsewhere are also worth looking at.*

The Quantocks (see pages 22-31)

These are a hill range about three miles in width and about twelve miles in length. Their tops are seldom higher than twelve hundred feet and are turf covered, with bracken, whortleberry and heather in plenty. The ponies that you are likely to see at some point along the tops are similar to those on Exmoor. A unique and very rare breed, they live wild, but are rounded up periodically into corrals, like the one at Point D, Map 9. Red deer were introduced from Exmoor in the 1860s and there are now about 800 in the Quantock area. However they tend to lie up in the daytime, either in woodlands or bracken, and unless you come here at dusk or the early morning you are unlikely to spot any. But do keep an eye open for buzzards, which are reasonably common here, and listen for their characteristic high-pitched mewing cry. Hopefully you will have already called in at the Fyne Court Visitor Centre (see page 24) and seen the displays illustrating the main features of the area.

Among the Quantocks' gentler eastern slopes, onto which our path does not intrude, are a series of beautifully wooded combes, almost all of which may be explored on foot. The spine track running north-westwards from the vicinity of Lydeard Hill almost to West Quantoxhead is well used at most times of the year. We therefore suggest that Macmillan Way West walkers avoid some of it by dropping down into Cothelstone and going just below the steep western slopes through West Bagborough and Triscombe before going up lovely Triscombe Combe to re-join it. From here Macmillan Way West follows the spine track, past Crowcombe Combe Gate and Halsway Post before finally dropping down into equally beautiful Bicknoller Combe.

West Somerset Railway (see page 32)

A revived 20-mile railway running between Bishops Lydeard and Minehead, with a bus link to Taunton from the former. Apart from the fascination of travelling in an old-style train (some steam-hauled) this line, with its intermediate stations near Crowcombe, Stogumber, Williton, Doniford, Watchet, Washford, Blue Anchor and Dunster, provides walkers with an invaluable facility. Tel: 01643 704996.

Sampford Brett (see page 32)

Small village in the valley of the Doniford stream with good views eastwards to the smooth flanks of the Quantocks, which we have recently left. The church has a stylish early-19th-century interior, the contents of which include a battered effigy, believed to be that of Richard de Brett, one of the four notorious knights who murdered Archbishop Becket in 1170. See also the bench-end commemorating the macabre story of Florence Wyndham, who is supposed to have come back to life only a short time before she was due to be buried in the family vault.

Williton (see page 33)

Busy little town with a wide selection of shops, inns, B&Bs and hotels that should prove invaluable to Macmillan Way Westers. The church, on our route just beyond the town, is largely Victorian, but it does include a fragment of a chantry chapel erected by his brother for the soul of Sir Reginald Fitzurse, the leader of the infamous gang of knights that murdered Archbishop Becket in 1170, another of whom was Richard de Brett (see above).

(A) Go straight over x-rds in Bicknoller, with useful Post Office shop over to right (but limited opening hours) (SP - *Williton*). Pass Village Hall with noticeboard on right and almost immediately go straight, not left at road junction with view of church down to left. Pass turning on left to Combe Close and soon leave Bicknoller. Go straight across busy A358 **with great care** and go up short surfaced roadway. Through large metal gate onto track straight ahead. At end of track disregard stile by large metal gate and stables, but turn right onto attractive, largely hidden path with overhanging bushes. When meeting metal gate ahead turn left to continue along narrow path with overhanging bushes. Over stile and **with very great care** cross line of the West Somerset Railway *(see page 31 for description). Wait long enough and you might see a fine steam-hauled train.* Over stile beyond railway line and through short, possibly overgrown area before veering right to go over stile. Go down field with hedge on immediate left. Through large metal gate passing farm buildings on left. Bear left through gateway and turn right onto farm road and pass Trenance Farm on right.

(B) Turn left with care onto fairly busy public road by Trenance farmhouse. Over bridge crossing the Doniford Stream and after 300 yards turn right at T-junction (SP - *Capton*). Almost immediately bear slightly right, off road keeping in same direction, onto track between two barns (SP - *Sampford Brett*). After about 350 yards, just beyond point where track starts to veer left, turn right just beyond large electricity pylon on right to go through kissing gate. Head straight across field, almost due north, aiming for kissing gate in hedge. Through this kissing gate in hedge and immediately turn left in bushy woodland before turning right to climb on path up wooded slope. Follow path as it gradually contours to left and then starts to drop down, with Doniford Stream down to right. Go quietly, straight in front of house on right. Keep along grassy driveway, running parallel to stream, and pass bungalow on right. Sampford Brett church tower visible ahead. Over stile beside metal gate and bear left through kissing gate at entry to Sampford Brett *(see page 31 for description).* Keep on road heading towards church and bear right at road junction by church on right *(no sign).* Keep up road out of village.

(C) Go over the busy A358 with **very great care** by the Quantock Service Station *(sweets, soft drinks, ice creams, etc)* and onto tarmac track to immediate left of main garage forecourt (SP - *Williton*). After 80 yards go between houses on both sides. On the right is Sampford Mill Farm, with the Doniford Stream beyond to right. Keep on now rougher track and over stile to left of large metal gate and keep on now grassy track. At end of wooded section of track bear left over stile and go along right-hand edge of field with ditch and hedge to immediate right. Over next stile to right of metal gate and still keep to right-hand edge of field. Through hinged

metal squeeze-stile and go along right-hand edge of next field. Through metal kissing gate and turn right onto short track before turning left onto surfaced road to enter Williton *(see page 31 for description).* By concrete parking area on left (reserved for bowling club) turn right and go along narrow surfaced pathway between houses *(no sign)* to emerge at narrow footbridge over stream. Pass bowling green and children's play area on right and games field on left. Through metal

At the Bakelite Museum

memorial gates and turn left with care onto busy A39, making sure to cross to opposite side. Pass White House Hotel and Royal Huntsman - both on right and bear left at first major road junction keeping on A39, using right-hand pavement. Pass Post Office on right with road almost opposite leading to toilets.

(D) Soon turn right, following A39 as it heads westwards. Immediately cross to opposite (left-hand) side of road, using traffic island. After 60 yards turn left onto minor road (SP - *The Bakelite Museum*). Bear right by triangular green (SP - *The Bakelite Museum*) and pass St Peter's Church on left.

(E) Bear right off road to go through small wooden gate beside cattle-grid (SP - *Yarde*). Go along tarmac driveway with stream just to left, and at second cattle-grid enter grounds of the Bakelite Museum and veer slightly right to go up across field with museum's boundary wall on left, aiming for hunting gate on edge of wood. *But first, do try to visit the interesting Bakelite Museum - with its fascinating and nostalgic displays of early plastic products on two floors of an old watermill, with much of its old mill machinery intact. Cream teas are also available!* Go through hunting gate and turn left to follow inner edge of woods. Through kissing gate at end of woods and keep along narrow path initially with hedges on both sides but emerging into left-hand edge of field. On meeting high wall ahead, turn left to go through hunting gate to right of large metal gate. Follow along right-hand edge of field with belt of trees on right - the remains of a driveway to the mansion of Orchard Wyndham. Through kissing gate and over attractive stone, single-arch footbridge crossing the remains of driveway and effectively turning right. Follow along left-hand edge of field with stream with weirs on immediate left. Over stile beside metal gate and keep in same direction following left-hand edge of another field.

(F) Over stile beside metal gate and bear slightly left to go on public road in Lower Stream hamlet, with driveway to Orchard Wyndham on left. Pass Stream Farm on right and turn right through small wooden gate immediately **before** road crosses Stream Bridge. Now following stream on left and soon pass Higher Stream Farmhouse on right.

(G) Follow next route directions with great care. Turn right onto tarmac farm road just beyond farmhouse and follow up initially well-surfaced farm road with wall to right. Pass waymark and bear slightly left around bottom left-hand edge of field, keeping parallel with overgrown, sunken track below to left. Turn right in bottom left-hand corner of field and keep up left-hand edge of field, ignoring track to left. Keep in same direction through field boundary at waymarked post, possibly obscured by summer vegetation. Keep in same direction in next field along its left-hand edge.

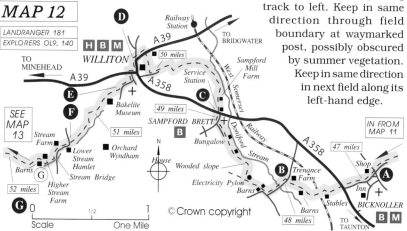

MAP 12

LANDRANGER 181
EXPLORERS OL9, 140

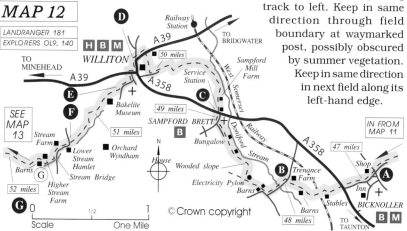

©Crown copyright

(A) On reaching brow, turn full right at waymarked post to go straight across field, aiming to left of left-hand radio mast visible in distance. At far side of field, go over waymarked stile and, keeping in same direction, go down right-hand edge of next field with hedge on immediate right. *Good view of Minehead's North Hill ahead left.* Turn left in bottom right-hand corner and soon turn right through gap to go with care onto reasonably busy public road (B3190). Turn right onto this road and almost immediately turn left through gap. Now turn left again and then turn right in top corner of field before going down left-hand edge with hedge on immediate left. Bear right in next corner and continue to follow down left-hand edge of field. Turn left at bottom left-hand corner (ignoring waymark), go through gap in hedge onto permissive path (probably not waymarked) and after about 200 paces, turn right through gap and then immediately left to go along parallel sunken track overhung with trees and fairly muddy. After about another 150 paces veer right ignoring remains of blocked-off trackway to go through or over wooden gate. Immediately veer left to go down left-hand edge of field with hedge and fence to immediate left. After about 100 yards veer left to go over wooden fence and go over stile just beyond. Now go down narrow pathway with hedge on left and wire fence of gravel depot on right. Pass in front of wire-mesh gates and continue along narrow concrete path. Bracken-covered slopes up to right and hedge on left. Over grassy area with bungalow up to right and veer slightly left into woodlands passing waymark post. Path partly obstructed by overhanging trees and nettles. Cross minor landslip with care and soon veer left to go down surfaced roadway.

(B) Turn left with care onto public road by Yew Tree Cottage (opposite) in Torre hamlet. *(But turn right and go along road for about 250 yards if you wish to call at the White Horse Inn, and/or go a further 600 yards beyond if you wish to visit the interesting ruins of 12th-15th-century Cleeve Abbey.)* Pass Torre House on left and turn right at road junction opposite 'The Coach House' *(no sign) (But go straight ahead if you wish to visit the Torre Cider Farm - on left after 100 yards - shop, ice creams, cream teas.)* Go up steep, narrow road ignoring bridleway coming in from left. Pass Beggearn Huish Farm, on left just beyond brow. Turn right at road junction just beyond postbox *(no sign)* and soon start losing height down steep, sunken lane overhung with trees to reach T-junction after 800 yards.

(C) Turn right at this T-junction *(no sign)* and pass Clitsome Farm on right. Over bridge crossing the Washford River at entry to Lower Roadwater and bear right onto wider and busier road *(no sign). (But turn left, go down road for half-a-mile, then turn left twice and go up road for another half-a-mile, if you*

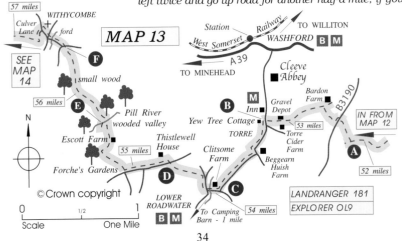

34

wish to stop at Woodavent Camping Barn.) Pass turning to Clitsome View on left and soon, at end of village, fork left onto narrower road (SP - *Rodhuish*). After 30 yards turn left up concrete steps (SP - *Footpath*) and go steeply up through small wood. Over stile, follow round bottom left-hand edge of field and **soon turn right** up short steep bank, ignoring path to left, to follow up left-hand edge of field with hedge to immediate

Track towards Escott Farm

left. At next corner of field, where hedge veers to right, go through gap beside disused stile and keep in same direction across next field. *Look back for good view of the Quantocks.*

(D) Over stile beside large metal gate and turn left onto public road. Ignore pathway on right down Thistlewell House's driveway. Bear right at road junction *(No sign)* where road to left is marked *Unsuitable for Heavy Vehicles.* Go gently downhill on road with oak trees on right. Turn right, off road (SP - *Withycombe)* at road junction at Forche's Gardens *(not signed as such)* onto track and then fork left a few paces beyond onto another track, which runs down right-hand edge of field. Follow track as it bends to right into belt of woodland and bear right again at cattle-grid just beyond wood and keep on track. Bear left on approaching Escott Farm's attractive farmhouse and keep on track to left of farm buildings. Bear left away from buildings and keep on track on right-hand edge of field with hedge to immediate right. Bear left keeping on track as it drops into wooded valley. Turn sharp right in valley to cross the little Pill River and follow track up far side. Turn left at exit from woodland and go up, straight across field. Head for wooden hunting gate in hedge ahead when it comes into view. Ignore stile to left and keep in about the same direction as before to go along left-hand edge of field with earth bank on immediate left. Bear left to keep along left-hand edge of field and through two large metal gates in quick succession. Go down field with hedge to immediate left - *sea visible over to right.*

(E) In valley bottom ignore gate on left and climb up far side with hedge still to immediate left. Through large metal gate into small wood and after about 35 yards veer right to aim for hunting gate on edge of wood. Go diagonally left across field, following waymark's direction aiming for hunting gate in hedge well ahead. Through this gate and keep in same direction across next field, aiming for wooden hunting gate soon seen in far hedge. *Minehead's North Hill visible well ahead.* Through this hunting gate and straight on following waymark direction. Then veer right, down field aiming for hunting gate in far hedge. Through this gate to veer left aiming for fingerpost and metal gate visible in far left-hand corner of field.

(F) Through metal gate and bear left onto public road by road junction, immediately going straight, not left. Go down sunken lane overhung by fine oak trees and enter Withycombe *(see page 36 for description).* Over footbridge beside ford and bear right at T-junction just beyond *(No sign).* Fork left (SP - *West Street*) passing white-painted church on right. After about 100 yards, take first turn left by One Elm Cottages to go up Culver Lane (SP - *Public Path to Dunster*). Soon turn right and keep up steep, roughly surfaced Culver Lane. **Now entering the Exmoor National Park; from here until leaving it near Brayford (page 49) any permitted waymarking has been carried out by the National Park with wooden signs inscribed MAC.**

Withycombe *(see page 35). We come beside a shallow ford into this pretty village sheltering in a small combe below the partly wooded Withycombe Hill. Before climbing up to this, on steep Culver Lane, try to find time to visit Withycombe's small 13th- and 14th-century colour-washed church. This has a circular Norman font, a fine 15th-century fan-vaulted screen, and below a window on the north side, the effigy of a man, who probably died some fifty years earlier than his lady. Both hold heart cases in their hands, possibly indicating that they were buried abroad, only their hearts being brought home for burial.*

(A) After nearly 500 yards go through kissing gate beside large metal gate onto open country. Continue on track across open country with grassland and gorse, *and fine views of coast over to right* and a glimpse of Dunster Castle ahead, down right. Keep on track, now with wire fence to immediate left. *Smooth, rounded Black Hill visible ahead left.* Through metal gate and keep in same direction, but now with fence to immediate right. Pass gorse-covered knoll on left and over rudimentary stile beside large metal gate. Now on wide track with scrubby country on both sides. Soon join better surfaced track coming in from right, gorse now on left, woodlands on right. This is the top of Withycombe Hill. At Y-junction veer slightly right, keeping to immediate left of woodlands - a pleasure to be walking on the level after our long climb up from Withycombe. *Splendid views ahead of the valley of the little River Avill, with Dunkery Beacon up to its left and the woodlands on Wootton Common above it to right.* Through large wooden gate keeping on track into coniferous woodlands. Fork right keeping on slightly wider track.

(B) At Aller Hill turn left at confusing junction of tracks in woodland and through small gate beside large wooden gate, signed *Withycombe Hill Gate* (SP - *Bridleway - Dunster*), but within a few paces, go straight, not right (SP - *Permitted Footpath to Bat's Castle*). **(But for shorter optional route,** *turn right (SP - Dunster) onto wide track leading more directly to Dunster. Keep on this track, ignoring smaller one to right. Also soon ignore faint path carrying straight on, as our track veers slightly to left. Keep on this track eventually bearing left by ancient oak trees. About 100 yards beyond oak trees turn right at a T-junction. Keep steeply downhill with stream eventually to left. Eventually go through wooden gate and soon bear left and over stile beside wooden gate* **rejoining main route at Point C1** *- see page 37.)*

On main route, having gone straight, not right, at Withycombe Hill Gate (see above), keep on track through coniferous woodlands, but after 150 yards emerge onto wide grassy track up through open, bracken- and heather-covered country. Path narrows (SP - *Ancient Monument - Cycles and horses prohibited*). Go across stony, south-eastern earthworks of Bat's Castle with great care ensuring that you do no damage. *This is a circular Iron Age hill fort bounded by two banks and a ditch.*

It dates from between 400 and 100BC and there are splendid all-round views from its high points. Pass interesting Bat's Castle information board on right and keep on path, now starting to descend with welcome bench not far beyond on left.

(C) After about 350 yards, at bottom of grassy pathway, turn down right (do **not** climb up straight ahead) *(No sign)*. Continue to drop down and after about 120 yards fork left onto narrow path that may be slightly overgrown *(No sign)*. Keep descending

Gallox Bridge - at our entry to Dunster

through thinned coniferous woodlands taking care to avoid partly hidden tree stumps.

(C1) Bear left into valley joining wider track (we are joined here by optional route) and keep down valley with bracken and increasing number of fine hardwood trees. Through hunting gate beside large wooden gate and keep on grassy track. Bear left and through kissing gate beside large wooden gate and almost immediately turn right at x-rds of tracks (SP - *Dunster*).

(D) Pass cottages on left and soon over medieval packhorse bridge - Gallox Bridge - over the little River Avill, with ford to right. At entry to Dunster go straight ahead onto tarmac path by car park on right (SP - *Mill Gardens*). Turn left at T-junction of paths *(but turn right if you wish to visit 18th-century Dunster Watermill, which has been restored to full working order)*. Up road with bungalows to left and small stream to right and turn right beyond 'The Old School House' onto busy A396. Go straight up road aiming towards church tower but turn up right (SP - *Dunster Castle*) onto roadway. *(If this is closed, keep straight on and then bear right with care along road to rejoin the preferred route beyond second set of traffic lights, where road turns left into the High Street.)* Pass toilets on right *(open at same time as castle)* and entrance to Dunster Castle on right just beyond. Turn left here and down roadway. At bottom of roadway go straight ahead, up Dunster's attractive High Street to arrive at the 17th-century Yarn Market, opposite the Luttrell Arms.

Dunster is an exceptionally picturesque little town, beautifully situated in the Avill valley, between Grabbist Hill, Castle Hill and, to its north, the smaller wooded Conygar Hill, which is topped by an 18th-century folly tower. This tower looks down Dunster's broad High Street, over the charming 17th-century Yarn Market and the Luttrell Arms, a pleasant hotel with several medieval features.

Dominating the far end of the High Street is the splendidly towered Dunster Castle, now, like the nearby watermill, in the hands of the National Trust. The castle was built on the site of a Saxon tower, but the earliest surviving structure is the 13th-century gatehouse. A Jacobean-style house was built within the walls, but as a Royalist stronghold the castle was largely demolished at the end of the Civil War. Today's highly romantic neo-medieval castle is mainly the result of remodelling in the 19th century by Anthony Salvin, best known for his massive rebuilding of Windsor Castle. Its interior is full of interest and there are splendid views across the Bristol Channel to the Welsh Coast. Dunster's church, originally part of a Benedictine priory, is now a fine, largely Perpendicular building. See especially the handsome tower, with its carillon bells, the splendid late-15th-century rood screen and the series of monuments to various members of the Luttrell family of Dunster Castle.

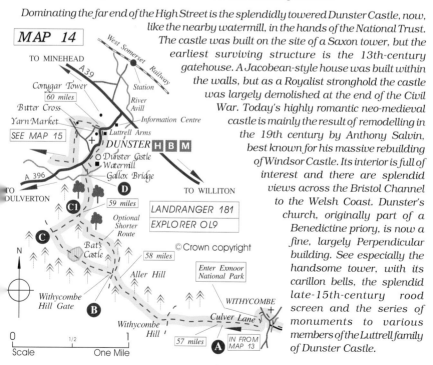

MAP 14

TO MINEHEAD

A39

West Somerset Railway

Conygar Tower
60 miles

Station

Butter Cross

River Avill

Yarn Market

Information Centre

SEE MAP 15

Luttrell Arms

DUNSTER H B M

Dunster Castle
Watermill

A 396

Gallox Bridge

TO DULVERTON

D

TO WILLITON

C1
59 miles

Optional Shorter Route

LANDRANGER 181

EXPLORER OL9

N

Bats Castle

58 miles

© Crown copyright

Aller Hill

Enter Exmoor National Park

Withycombe Hill Gate

B

WITHYCOMBE

Culver Lane

Withycombe Hill

57 miles

IN FROM MAP 13

A

0   1/2   1
Scale   One Mile

37

(A) Leave Dunster's Yarn Market northwards with the Luttrell Arms on right, almost immediately going up narrow pathway with walls on both sides. *(But bear right along road beyond the Luttrell Arms if you wish to visit the very helpful Exmoor National Park Information Centre - and then return to the narrow pathway.)* Turn left onto narrow road and beyond Conygar House go straight ahead onto path with tall garden wall on left and fenced field to right (SP - *Butter Cross*). Go through wooden kissing gate and keep in same direction across field. Through small wooden gate and pass medieval Butter Cross on left. Turn left with care onto public road (St George's Street) and soon turn right at road junction. Almost immediately fork left onto metalled road (Hanger's Way). At end of road go through wooden kissing gate and pass allotments to right. Go through wooden gate (SP - *Bridleway*), leaving cemetery to left. Keep just outside right-hand edge of cemetery *(fine views of Dunster back left)* to further wooden gate at top of corner. Through gate and take leftmost of three tracks (SP - *Selworthy*). Go down hill for about 50 yards to Y-junction of tracks and fork right. Now following steep, right-hand side of Avill Valley, rising gently towards top of Grabbist Hill. After a short, steep section arrive at top of Grabbist Hill *(NT Sign)*.

(B) Turn left by Grabbist Hill National Trust sign on right *(But go straight over if you are staying at the Alcombe Youth Hostel - about half-a-mile ahead)*. Soon emerge onto open moorland country going along a gradually rising ridge with fine views over to left of the slopes of Dunkery Beacon and of Minehead including Butlin's with its unmissable white 'tented' roof down to the right. Beyond, in the distance the coastline of South Wales is also visible on a clear day. Follow path carefully as it bends slightly to right and soon ignore small left-hand fork. Pass another path coming in from right and fork right by seat in memory of Gary Draper (SP - *Bridleway - Selworthy*). Open country to right, woods to left - path almost level. Now enter woodland again and ignore good track down to right. Keep straight ahead ignoring trackway coming in from left.

(C) At x-rds of tracks by picnic area on right, go straight ahead on main route (SP - *Selworthy and Wootton Courtenay*) turning to Point A on Map 16 - at top of page 40). **But turn right (SP - *Minehead)*) if you wish to go down to Minehead to link onto the South-West Coast Path, and use the following route directions.** Keep straight down the best of the sandy tracks, not turning right on path just beyond picnic area.   Follow gently curving track down through pleasant woodlands. Fork left, keeping on higher of two tracks, soon passing bench on right. Track now more stony than sandy. Turn left onto top end of surfaced public road by small car park and continue to go downwards through woodlands on this, now watching out for cars. Pass Higher Hopcott (farm) up to left. **Cross very busy relief road with great care** at Lower Hopcott and go

Dunster

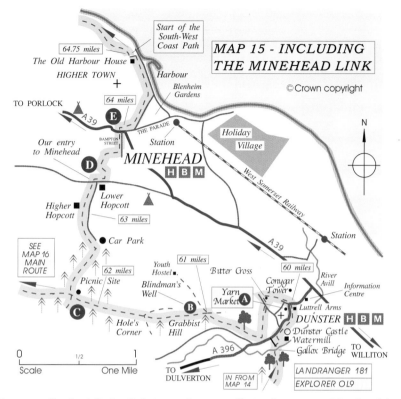

MAP 15 - INCLUDING THE MINEHEAD LINK

© Crown copyright

Start of the South-West Coast Path

64.75 miles

The Old Harbour House ■

HIGHER TOWN

Harbour

Blenheim Gardens

64 miles

TO PORLOCK

A39

THE PARADE

Our entry to Minehead

BAMPTON STREET

Station

MINEHEAD H B M

Holiday Village

West Somerset Railway

N

Lower Hopcott

Higher Hopcott ■

63 miles

Car Park

Station

SEE MAP 16 MAIN ROUTE

62 miles

Picnic Site

61 miles

Youth Hostel ■

Butter Cross

60 miles

Conygar Tower ●

River Avill

Information Centre

A39

Blindman's Well

Yarn Market A

Luttrell Arms

DUNSTER H B M

C

Hole's Corner

Grabbist Hill

B

A 396

Dunster Castle

Watermill

Gallox Bridge

TO WILLITON

0 · 1/2 · 1

Scale   One Mile

TO DULVERTON

IN FROM MAP 14

LANDRANGER 181

EXPLORER OL9

down small, short footpath between houses, effectively entering Minehead *(not signed)*.

(D) Go straight over road, bend round to right and almost immediately turn left along another path between houses. Go straight across road and along another path, which is initially a road for about five yards. Pass allotments on left-hand side and at end of path turn right to go down road (no name showing at this point). Turn left onto busier road passing shop on left and a telephone box on left (this is Bampton Street). Now follow down to end of Bampton Street before turning right with care into busier Park Street.

Minehead is a bright and cheerful holiday resort town with many helpful shops, a two-mile long sand and pebble beach and a massive holiday village on its eastern side. It does however have quieter corners to offer. Quay Town has a long row of fishermen's cottages and beyond these is a small harbour. Above this is Higher Town with its steep streets leading up to a handsomely towered 15th-century grey stone church. Inside this will be found a fine 15th-century rood screen, an elegant Perpendicular font and a Jacobean pulpit.

(E) Go along Park Street and continue in same direction along The Parade at the centre of Minehead. Now turn left into Blenheim Road, with Blenheim Gardens to right. At the end of gardens bear half right into Quay Lane before turning left into Quay Street, with the sea now on right and the harbour ahead. After about 200 yards go left up steps just beyond The Old Harbour House on left. After a few yards turn right onto path signed *Coast Path*, complete with a map of the South-West Coast Path and an unusual sculpture. **Good Luck with the rest of your walk!**

West from Dunkery

(A) Go over x-rds (SP - *Selworthy and Wootton Courtenay*) which were referred to as **Point C on page 38**, and continue to climb up track with woodlands on left and open moorland to right. Continue for about 300 yards to oblique track crossroads (*unsigned*). Cross oblique track, keeping in same direction as before for a further 600 yards.

(B) Turn left at cross-roads of tracks (SP - *Wootton Courtenay*). *(From this point until reaching the end of woodlands, the directions look very complex, but take heart, they should not prove too difficult if taken one at a time!)* Immediately bear left through gap in bank and turn right to follow down track with woods on right. After 300 yards fork left at Y-junction (SP - *Footpath*) and after a further 200 yards go straight, not right at Y-junction leaving wider track and down steep, narrower track. Bear right and cross wide forestry track, keeping down in same direction following path below beech trees (SP - *Wootton Courtenay*). After about 50 yards turn left down steep path and then bear right onto wider track, still dropping down. Cross wider track and cross another one diagonally just beyond. Over stile at end of woodlands and keep in same direction down across field aiming for stile and gate to right of houses. *Note vineyard on slopes just over to right.* Good view of Dunkery ahead - quite a climb!

(C) Over stile and keep in same direction down public road entering Wootton Courtenay **being careful of traffic.** *Wootton Courtenay has a useful shop which was saved from closure by the joint action of the villagers some years ago. The nearby church dates from the 13th century and its contents include canopied niches in the north arcade pillars and some fine bosses to the roofs of the nave and north aisle.* Keep through village going straight, not left, and passing shop on right **(do make use of it)**, with church up to right. Pass Dunkery Beacon Hotel on right and at 4-way road junction, turn left over stile beside wooden gate (SP - *Footpath - Ford 1m*). Now go slightly left, down across field. Go over stile, drop down to cross sunken trackway and up to go over opposite stile. Go along left-hand edge of cricket field, turning right in rougher part of field for a few yards before turning left to return to same direction with hedge still on left. Over stile with power-pole just to right and keep in same direction across next field aiming for stile at left-hand end of cross-hedge. Over this stile (possibly signed *Please do not feed pony*) and keep in same direction across large field aiming just to left of small clump of trees. Pass to immediate left of trees and over stile in right-hand corner. Go up short, narrow pathway with fence to left and hedge to right and over stile. Go up field keeping to its right-hand edge and over stile beside metal gate.

(D) Turn left onto public road. After about 40 yards turn right onto rough track (SP - *Dunkery*). Go up track with bracken on both sides (now back in National Trust area) and fork left at Y-junction of tracks dropping slightly down to beautiful woodlands - young oaks, silver birch, beech. Fork right at next junction of

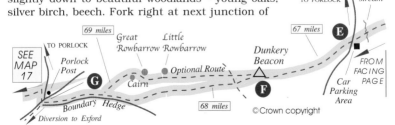

tracks into older woodland with banks above track. Turn left at junction of tracks (SP - *Dunkery*) now going up more steeply and at exit from woodlands go straight, not left (SP - *Dunkery Beacon - 2*). Now climbing path through open moorland with fine views back over the Avill Valley. Do not be put off by false brow - the top of this path is further ahead than you might imagine - but it will all be worthwhile! Follow path as it veers to right and soon levels out for a time. Cross very small stream and follow main path as it bears slightly left and resumes a steady climb.

(**E**) Go over public road with care, with cars possibly parked to your left, and go on broad, well-used track, still climbing (SP - *Dunkery Beacon*). Dunkery Beacon soon visible ahead, slightly right and track levels out - please keep to this main track, from which there are fine views southwards. Track begins to climb again and keep on this as it gently curves to right.

(**F**) Arrive at Dunkery Beacon - *at 1707 feet above sea-level, this is the highest point on the Macmillan network. From its bracken- and heather-covered slopes, there are splendid views northwards to the wooded combes of Holnicote and to the sea at Porlock Bay; south to the gentle valleys of the Barle and Exe; east to the Brendons and the Quantocks, and west towards the central massif of Exmoor itself, where the Badgworthy, Barle, Lyn and Exe all have their source. On a clear day the heights of Dartmoor and Bodmin, the Mendips and the Brecon Beacons may all be seen on the distant skyline and the reasons for Dunkery's use as a beacon point over the centuries are then abundantly clear. The large cairn on the summit was built in 1935 to commemorate the donation of the area to the National Trust.* **Normally (see below*)** go on wide, well-defined track, west-south-westwards, meeting boundary hedge coming in from left. Continue in same direction keeping on track to immediate right of boundary hedge. After one-and-a-quarter miles, arrive at public road junction at Porlock Post (identified on signpost). *(*If weather is fine you may prefer to take an optional route, by walking almost due westward on right-hand of two tracks leaving Dunkery Beacon, going to the immediate left of the Bronze Age cairns of Little and Great Rowbarrow (4000 - 3500 BC), visible on skyline ahead. Beyond third cairn veer left (WSW) to re-join main route.)*

(**G**) Turn **half-right** onto road at Porlock Post and immediately fork left at Y-junction. **(But bear fully left here, down road and follow for 500 yards if you wish to divert to Exford - see Map 17 and text on page 42 for further details of this diversion.)** On main route, having turned half-right and forked left at Porlock Post (SP *Stoke Pero*), follow road for about 300 yards. Take waymarked, but ill-defined track to left at small square, standing stone - this is point A on Map 17.

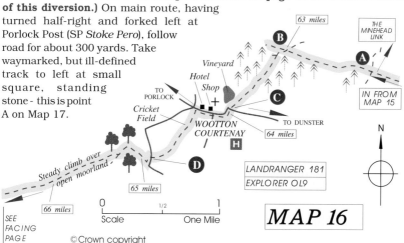

THE MINEHEAD LINK

63 miles

B

A

IN FROM MAP 15

Vineyard

Hotel

Shop

TO PORLOCK

C

Cricket Field

WOOTTON COURTENAY

TO DUNSTER

64 miles

H

D

65 miles

Steady climb over open moorland

66 miles

LANDRANGER 181

EXPLORER OL9

N

0   1/2   1
Scale   One Mile

MAP 16

SEE FACING PAGE

©Crown copyright

41

Exford *(2 miles from Main Route at Porlock Post) - A possible diversion for supplies, accommodation and meals. This starts from Point G, near the bottom of page 41, where it is necessary to go down road south-westwards from Porlock Post for 500 yards before turning left onto a track and soon bearing right onto bridleway. Exford is a pleasant village on the River Exe and overlooked by high moorland on almost every side. It has a hotel, inn, youth hostel and shops, and camping facilities close by (see map). It would be possible to return to our route by using minor roads as far as Larkbarrow Corner, Point D.*

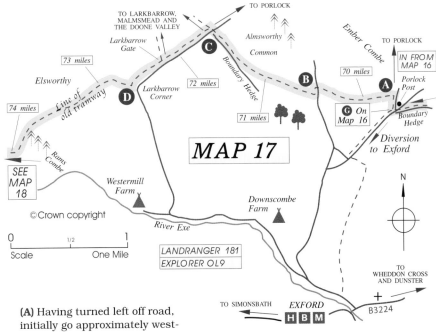

(A) Having turned left off road, initially go approximately westwards following ill-defined track, boggy in places, and becomes a slightly narrower path through tussocky grass. Follow path as it curves slightly left and then right, keeping approximately to the contour and changing direction to north-westwards. *Fine views down Ember Combe to right.* Follow what is now a track as it starts to rise a little with views down right to the sea and across to the Welsh coast.

(B) Turn left with care onto public road and after almost 200 yards turn right, off road and down track (SP - *In the interests of conservation no vehicles beyond this point*). Follow this good surfaced track but after 200 yards go straight ahead at Y-junction leaving better-used track and drop down on grassy track to cross Almsworthy Common, with *fine views over to left including the smooth-shaped Withypool Common*. At junction of tracks in lowest part of common veer onto less defined, left-hand track. Now gradually veer up left to join hedgerow coming in from our left. Bear right onto grassy track with hedge on immediate left and follow this track, with heather- and bracken-covered Almsworthy Common to right and pasture field over to left.

(C) At end of track turn left onto public road and through gate if you wish to avoid cattlegrid, but make sure it is firmly closed. *(It is possible to go straight over road*

42

at this point to go north-westwards to Larkbarrow, Malmsmead and the Doone Valley.) Having turned left walk down road with care for almost three-quarters of a mile. Pass sign on right at Larkbarrow Gate to Larkbarrow Boundary Walk.

(D) After a further 450 yards, where road bends to left at Larkbarrow Corner, turn right through hunting gate beside large wooden gate and go up track (SP - *Bridleway to Simonsbath*). At top of slope bear left and go through hunting gate beside large wooden gate (SP (possibly vandalised) - *Simonsbath via Warren Farm*). Initially bear right and follow up wall and fence line to immediate right, but after about 50 yards bear left following slight signs of track, which are the scanty remains of a partly built, but never completed tramway constructed by the Knights for the transport of iron ore. Being the remains of a tramway, this track closely follows the contour (just above 1400 feet) and is easy to identify. Good views down left into the Exe Valley with lovely rounded green slopes - some pasture, some wild. Across boggy stretch of track and soon pass fence line and trees coming up from Ram's Combe on left. Follow track as it climbs slightly and first bends to left following boundary bank and fence on left. Keep on track as it now takes a long, gentle bend to right following boundary fence and bank on immediate left. Eventually track resumes a straight, almost westerly direction, with boundary bank and fence on left.

EXMOOR (See Pages 36 - 48)

The Exmoor National Park, with only 265 square miles within its boundaries, is one of Britain's smaller National Parks, but it contains such a variety of coast and countryside that its very compactness becomes one of its greatest assets. The wilder heather moorland, which is itself lighter and more colourful than its neighbour to the south, Dartmoor, is broken by gentle valleys pushing up from the south, and short torrential streams flowing quickly, often in the company of great tracts of woodland, off steep northern slopes into the sea. The high moorland, much of which we cross, is interspersed by the farms established in the heart of Exmoor by the Knight family of Simonsbath (see page 45) but this softening process has in a mysterious way added to, rather than detracted from, Exmoor's subtle appeal. Everywhere one looks out towards long moorland horizons, with farmland and wooded valleys relieving any possible monotony in the middle distance, and with luck, there may be shafts of sunlight striking out of low cloud-scattered skies, illuminating parts of this magic landscape. Ponies, red deer and soaring buzzards are to be seen by those who move quietly and keep their eyes well open.

Often glorious, Exmoor's weather can easily change for the worse, so do be prepared especially when moving away from the roads on the long stretches between Dunkery and Mole's Chamber (see page 7 for further advice).

A short pause at Porlock Post (see page 41)

(A) Through hunting gate beside large wooden gate. *If you are using the Ordnance Survey's Explorer Map of Exmoor, this is the point where you have to turn to the reverse side - Good luck with this operation - let's hope that you have less wind than the original route planner, when he tried this trick!* Soon bear left through hunting gate beside large wooden gate and keep down track with fence and bank on immediate right. Through large metal gate and keep on track, soon crossing stream. Bear left at Y-junction of tracks just beyond and go through hunting gate beside large wooden gate and go straight ahead onto Warren Farm's tarmac road which soon bends down to right and drops down into the Exe Valley *(but turn right towards farmyard if you are planning to stay at Warren Farm). Warren Farm was one of the Knight farmsteads (see Simonsbath and Exmoor Forest - page 45) and was known as such because of the rabbit warrens, the mounds of which can still be seen from our path beyond here.* Bend round to left to go over bridge crossing the River Exe and after about 50 yards turn right and follow steep path (SP - Bridleway to Cloven Rocks). *Known locally as The Postman's Path, this is a steep and, at times, slippery pathway and should, in our opinion, be tackled slowly - those postmen must have been a tough breed!* Initially disregard the fingerpost direction and go up stony path, although this soon veers to right to follow the general direction of the fingerpost. Follow path as it zig-zags up steep hillside and spare time for views back, down the Exe Valley.

(B) At top of path turn right to follow to immediate right of bank and fence, initially heading north-westwards with the headwaters of the River Exe roughly parallel in valley well down to our right. Through large wooden gate and continue to immediate right of fence. Disregard footpath sign pointing diagonally right and keep along fence line which starts to veer to left. Through hunting gate in cross fence and bank and turn left (southwards) with fence and bank now on immediate left. *(If, and only if, the weather is clear, and the ground not too boggy and you don't wish to divert to Simonsbath, you could go straight ahead here, aiming directly west to join the B3223 at Preyway Head - Point D.)* After about 400 yards turn right (westwards) in field corner ignoring gates ahead and on left. After about 300 yards pass gate on left still heading westwards, with views of Simonsbath in Barle valley to left.

(C) After a further 400 yards keep straight ahead (SP -*Preyway*) passing gate on left. *(But if you wish to divert to Simonsbath, turn left through gate onto permissive path (SP - Simonsbath) passing sheep pens on right and heading slightly east of south with field boundary joining on right. Follow faint path until small clump of trees with gate to right becomes visible in distance. After about*

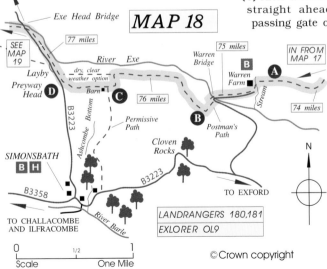

MAP 18

TO LYNMOUTH

Exe Head Bridge

SEE MAP 19

77 miles

River Exe

Layby

dry, clear weather option

Preyway Head **D**

Barn

C

B3223

Ashcombe Bottom

76 miles

Permissive Path

Cloven Rocks

SIMONSBATH

B **H**

B3358

B3223

TO CHALLACOMBE AND ILFRACOMBE

River Barle

0   1/2   1
Scale   One Mile

Warren Bridge

75 miles

B

Warren Farm ■

A

Stream

74 miles

B

Postman's Path

N

TO EXFORD

LANDRANGERS 180,181
EXLORER OL9

© Crown copyright

400 yards cross low hedge by waymark and turn left following path over small bridge. Follow path swinging right to gate with beech hedge to left. Through gate and go across middle of field to waymark before heading towards telegraph pole, picking up waymark to its left. Follow path beyond waymark contouring to left around slope to arrive at hunting gate. Through this gate into woodland, turning half-left to cross small brook and climb south-eastwards with sheep fence to left. Follow path to right with hedge/fence on left into wood. Follow path until it begins to descend towards buildings in valley, finally emerging into small car park. Follow lane to road and turn right onto this for Exmoor Forest Hotel and Cafe.)

Climbing the Postman's Path

Back on main route just beyond (C), continue straight on with hedge and fence on left, towards small cement-rendered barn. Pass to right of barn and continue parallel to hedge, about 30 yards to left. After about 200 yards ignore gate to left and continue with hedge/fence, which begins to veer to right, now heading north-westwards aiming for hunting gate a few yards to right of large wooden gate in roadside field boundary.

(D) Through hunting gate and turn right **with care** onto B3223 to the north of Preyway Head and go along wide verge on right-hand side of this often busy road for about 300 yards. Pass layby on left - **this is (A) at top of page 46**. If the weather is really clear it is possible to take a short-cut to Exe Head, turning left from this layby and going over Dure Down, thus avoiding the rest of B3223.

Simonsbath and Exmoor Forest - *situated at the very heart of Exmoor, this minute village, with its two hotels, cafe and pottery, shelters in the valley of the Barle and is overlooked by hillsides planted with larch and fir. It appears to have been the centre of the Royal Forest of Exmoor since Norman times, the word forest indicating that this was a hunting preserve, rather than a large area of woodland. Exmoor*

Forest covered a relatively small proportion of the present National Park's area and in the 17th century Simonsbath House was built by James Boevey, the Forest Warden after the Commonwealth period. In 1818 all the remaining royal interests were offered for sale, and most of the land was purchased by John Knight, a prosperous Worcestershire iron-master. Vast sums were spent by John and later by his son, Frederick, upon the reclamation of great tracts of derelict moorland, with the creation of roads, boundary walls and tall beech hedges and the establishment of extensive grazing lands. Sadly Frederick's only son died in 1879 and not long afterwards he sold his lands to the Lord Fortescue, whose family had been Devonshire landowners for many generations. Most of the Fortescues' Exmoor holdings have been sold off and fragmented but much of the pattern of today's Exmoor farming is still due to the persistent pioneer work of the Knights.

Exe Head Bridge

45

(A) Keep down right-hand side of B3223 for almost three-quarters of a mile and then turn left off road just before reaching Exe Head Bridge (SP - *Exe Head*). To avoid boggy ground make sure to take path up bank well to left of the infant Exe. Path soon levels out and starts to follow contour parallel with the Exe. Over stile (SP - *Exe Head*) and after some time veer left (SP - *Exe Head*) to follow fenceline, now on immediate right. Rising all the way, follow fenceline for about 500 yards.

(B) Soon arrive at 4-way fingerpost at Exe Head, which, like many sources, is not very impressive. However it is an important junction of paths where we cross the Two Moors Way and join the Tarka Trail. *Crossing much of Exmoor and Dartmoor, The Two Moors Way is a 104-mile long-distance path running between Lynmouth on the North Devon coast and Ivybridge on the southern fringes of Dartmoor. The Tarka Trail follows a complex route around much of North Devon and endeavours to relate the scenery and modern landscape to that depicted in Henry Williamson's delightful classic tale,* Tarka the Otter. *We shall follow the Tarka Trail initially for a short distance and, a little later, for many miles, between Mole's Chamber and Barnstaple.* Path to north and south-west is the Two Moors Way and crosses our own route. Also coming in from the north and sharing the Two Moors Way is the Tarka Trail, but this now heads generally westwards and, for the moment, we shall follow it for the next one-and-a-quarter miles. Therefore go straight ahead (SP - *Pinkery Pond*) ignoring gate on right and now keep on broad track with fence on immediate right. Through large wooden gate (SP - *Pinkery Pond*) and continue on track with fenceline on right. Pass SP - *Pinkery Pond and Chains Barrow*. Good views to left over the Barle Valley. Pass gate on right and continue to follow embankment topped by fenceline on immediate right, heading approximately north-westwards. *This embankment was known as Paddy's Fence as it was built by Irish labourers working for John Knight.* Keep in same direction through large wooden gate. Chains Barrow trig point now visible ahead right. Over head of small stream by stepping stones and after about 400 yards arrive at small gate on right with 4-way fingerpost. *Walk up to right here for 300 yards if you wish to visit Bronze Age Chains Barrow, which at 1598 feet above sea level is only 109 feet lower than Dunkery Beacon. On a clear day it is possible to see Hartland Point and Lundy Island from here. The extensive area to the north of the barrow is known as The Chains and is some of the wildest and least accessible land in the Park. As such it was much loved by Henry Williamson, who often walked here, and he describes Tarka's visit to it in* Tarka the Otter. *Pinkery Pond, about half-a-mile ahead of this path junction, was created by John Knight by damming the infant River Barle, which rises just to its north.*

(C) Turn left at this 4-way fingerpost leaving the Tarka Trail for the moment (SP - *Bridleway B3358 road*) and head approximately south-westwards across open moorland, dropping down gently and following a line of marker posts. After about

Our path down towards Lew Combe

400 yards veer slightly left to head southwards somewhere near the crossing of a drainage or boundary ditch. Go through large wooden gate well to right of hunting gate and veer left into rough field to walk as near as possible to bank and fence on its left-hand side. At bottom left-hand corner of field go through gate straight ahead. Keep down field soon dropping steeply with boundary hedge to left.

(D) Through hunting gate and **turn left with care onto B3358 and use left-hand verge**. We are now in the valley of the River Barle heading eastwards. The River Barle has its

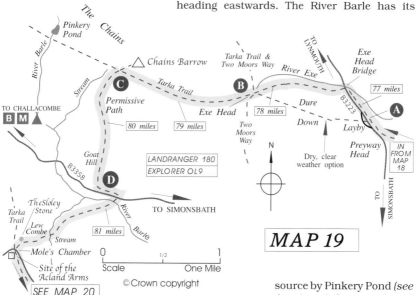

source by Pinkery Pond (*see above*) and flows east and south-east to join the Exe just below Dulverton. After about 350 yards **cross B3358 with great care** and turn sharp right to go through gate on surfaced farm drive (*SP - Mole's Chamber*). Keep on driveway crossing the infant River Barle and at top of first slope beyond bridge, bear right, off track as it turns to left. Through large wooden gate (*SP - Bridleway*) and keep up hill on broad slightly sunken, grassy trackway. Through large wooden gate in cross-fence and, ignoring possible track veering to left, go slightly to right, on narrow pathway initially above edge of deep little Lew Combe down to right and eventually drop down into combe. Cross stream at foot of minor combe coming in from left and bear to right to keep in 'our' combe. Now going beside beech hedge which comes in from right. *This hedge is probably one of the many hundreds of hedges planted by Frederick Knight. Judging from its structure, it must be over 150 years old and has been 'laid' many times.* Just beyond end of beech hedge turn right through hunting gate, ford small stream near head of combe and up small bank with low wall to immediate right. At top of bank cross field in same direction and through large wooden gate. *Pass the Sloley Stone, up to right, erected further to the north in 1742, to mark the boundary between High Bray Common and Gratton Manor Common. The Lady of the latter manor was Christian Sloley.* Almost immediately through large metal gate and pass corrugated shed on left to arrive at minor public road at Mole's Chamber (*not indicated*). *There appears to be no explanation for this intriguing place-name. One can only assume that there must have been a local farmer named Mole - but who knows?*

(A) Bear left onto minor public road where it turns sharply at Mole's Chamber (*no indication here*). *Note enclosure in angle of road opposite - this is the site of a sadly long-vanished inn - The Acland Arms- once very popular with the Welsh and Cornish miners employed in the area by Frederick Knight and others.* Go up and along road for about one-and-a-half miles. This carries very little traffic and there are some splendid views over to the right of rolling Devonshire countryside and Barnstaple Bay. *Note three attractive seats on right of road between (A) and (B), the first, appropriately, with a mole carved upon it.* If in doubt follow Tarka Trail waymarks, although Macmillan Way waymarks should be in place once we leave the Exmoor National Park (towards the end of paragraph C).

(B) Turn right off road and go through metal gate (SP - *Whitefield*) effectively leaving the moor and keep down right-hand side of field with fence to immediate right passing tumulus on left and then, in the adjoining field, one on right - *these, like the cairns on the moor, are almost certainly Bronze Age burial mounds.* Now starting to drop down off the high country, veer left to keep on track to go through large wooden gate. Keep straight across next field going parallel with fence well to our right, but towards bottom of field veer to right and go through large metal gate. Ignore second gate just beyond and go down next field to immediate right of fence line. At x-rds of fences go straight ahead over stile beside metal gate (SP - *Whitfield - Lower Hall*). Do not follow fence line to left, but go diagonally right, across field keeping in same direction as previously. Over stile beside metal gate and go straight ahead down field keeping to right-hand side of fence on left. Over stile in cross-fence. At bottom of field follow track as it veers off right from fenceline and leaves field. Through small ford with pond below oak tree to its right and go down concrete farm drive. Through gate or over cattle-grid by barns and veer left onto beginning of minor public road. Keep on road through Whitefield hamlet and down steep lane.

(C) Immediately beyond point where lane turns sharp right, turn left through large wooden gate *(SP - Lower Hall)* and immediately over stile beside second wooden gate. Immediately beyond this and **well before third gate** turn right off track and go down steep bank **before** reaching third gate. Through hunting gate at bottom left-hand

Valley just beyond Whitefield. (Go down steep bank to right just **before** this point)

side of field and across small field with fence on immediate right and go over footbridge crossing Little Owl River. Bear left up small slope to go over stile into large wood. Up steep but pleasant path through woodlands with stream sometimes visible through trees well down to left. Path soon levels out and after about 400 yards keep straight ahead at junction of path and track coming in from right. Path becomes farm lane and immediately before metal gate ahead, turn left to go down small path parallel to our now very muddy farm lane. Bear left to go over stile and turn right onto minor public road which here runs along boundary of the Exmoor National Park. Go along road for about 100 yards, pass farm down to left and continue on road for about another 700 yards.

(D) Now **turn left** onto a quieter road leading to High Bray **(leaving the Exmoor National Park)**.

Tarka Trail

The Sloley Stone

A

IN FROM MAP 19

82 miles

Site of the Acland Arms

Bronze Age Burial Mounds

83 miles

B

84 miles

LANDRANGER 180

EXPLORER OL9

WHITEFIELD

Small pond

© Crown copyright

C

85 miles

Little Owl River

Leave Exmoor National Park

MAP 20

D

Whitebeam

BRAYFORD

86 miles

HIGH BRAY

Scale 0 ——— 1/2 ——— 1 One Mile

N

TO ILFRACOMBE

River Bray

87 miles

A399

Rocks Head Cross

E

SEE MAP 21

Newtown Bridge

TO SOUTH MOLTON

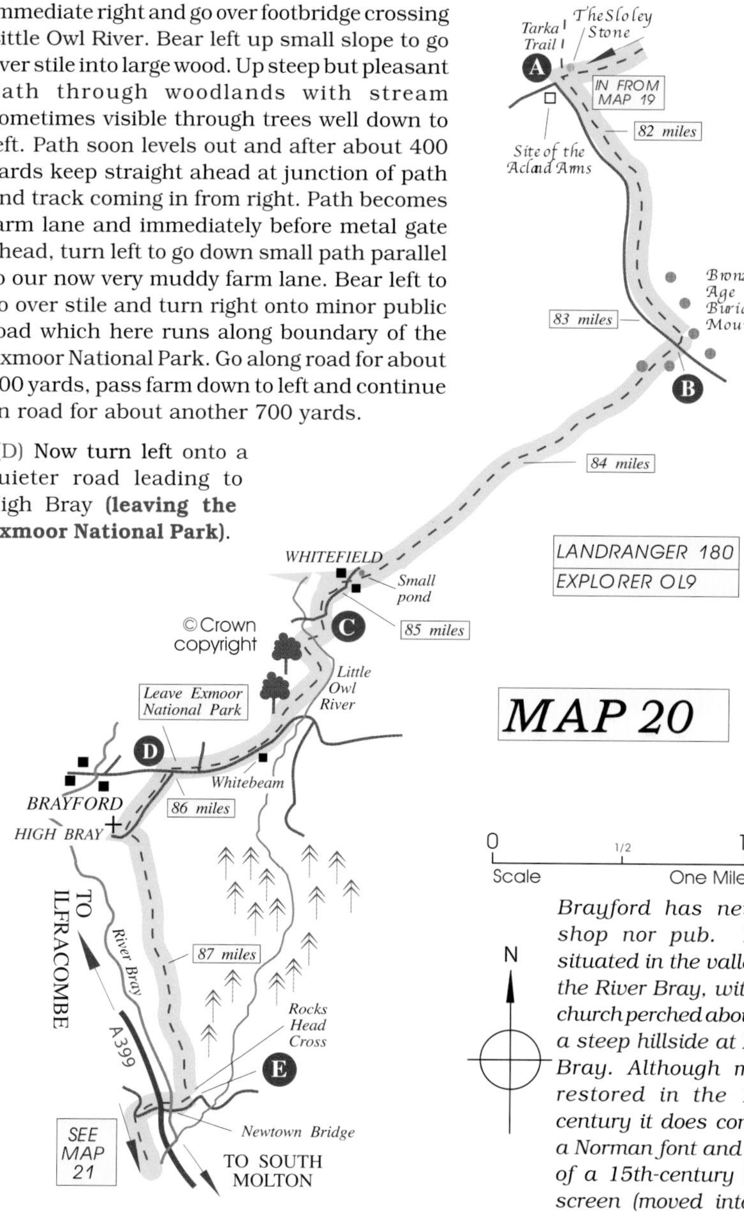

Brayford has neither shop nor pub. It is situated in the valley of the River Bray, with its church perched above on a steep hillside at High Bray. Although much restored in the 19th century it does contain a Norman font and part of a 15th-century rood screen (moved into its tower arch). At entry to High Bray, opposite High Bray Farm, turn left. Almost immediately turn left again to go down Barton Lane (SP - *Unsuitable for Motor Vehicles*). After bending to the right, keep on this `byway open to all traffic` for just over a mile, firstly through fields, and then through woodlands.

(E) Just after a sharp left bend emerge at Rocks Head Cross and turn right to go onto minor road (SP - *Brayford*).

Autumn in Reapham Wood

(A) Over Newtown Bridge crossing the River Bray and bear slightly right to cross the busy, bendy A399 **with very great care** onto minor public road (SP - *Charles Bottom*). Up steep hill and where road bends sharply to right, turn left in front of house called Grass Park (SP - *Tarka Trail*). Immediately beyond house turn left down surfaced driveway with stone bungalow on immediate right and over stile below oak tree. Go straight down (south-eastwards) across field and over stile beside large wooden gate. Veer right down stony pathway between hedges. Over small ford and turn half-right to go through large wooden gate and along grassy track into extensive Reapham Wood. Over possible stile and try to avoid possibly boggy area by veering right onto an upper path, soon following parallel with River Bray to our left. Re-join wider, lower path now beside the River Bray - a very attractive stretch, but probably very wet after rain. Pass small stone barn on left, with River Bray now some distance to left. Through gateway at point where the Bray comes closer to us again. *This journey from the heights of Exmoor to the Bray Valley is one of delightful contrasts - wide open skies beneath heather clad moors, gentle farming valleys and deep woodlands.* Go up better used track to climb out of valley and through gateway at top of slope and onto muddy lane between hedges. Through gate by barn on right, through large metal gates and soon - - -

(B) Turn right with care onto minor public road and after a few yards turn left at road junction in minute hamlet of West Blakewell. Go along this delightful and very quiet minor road. This is a side valley following a tributary of the River Bray which is down

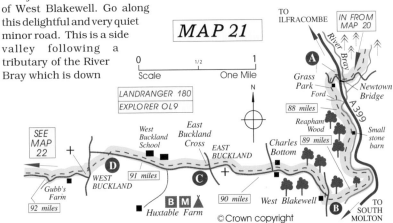

MAP 21

TO ILFRACOMBE

IN FROM MAP 20

River Bray

Scale 0 — 1/2 — 1 One Mile

LANDRANGER 180
EXPLORER OL9

N

A

Grass Park
Ford
Newtown Bridge

88 miles

Reapham Wood

Small stone barn

89 miles

SEE MAP 22

West Buckland School
East Buckland Cross
EAST BUCKLAND

Charles Bottom

D

WEST BUCKLAND
91 miles

C

Gubb's Farm

92 miles

B M
Huxtable Farm

90 miles   West Blakewell

B

TO SOUTH MOLTON

© Crown copyright

50

to the left. Fork left in hamlet of Charles Bottom (SP - *East Buckland*) and over bridge crossing stream. Up steep lane passing modern barns to right. Enter East Buckland climbing steadily and bear right in village and then immediately bear left with church on left. *East Buckland is a small village with no inn or shop. Its church was re-built in 1860, utilising the tower of a previous building, in the west side of which is a bricked-up Norman doorway.*

The Bray Valley near West Blakewell

(C) Over x-rds at East Buckland Cross with great care (SP - *West Buckland*). **Walk with care - this road now busier, especially at the beginning and end of the day, owing to the presence of West Buckland School.** Pass driveway on left leading to Huxtable Farm (B&B and camping) and almost immediately pass impressive West Buckland School on right.

(D) About 600 yards beyond the school, turn left by wide parking area on left and through large wooden gates (SP - *Tarka Trail*). Go up across field diagonally right aiming for church tower, but veer slightly left in middle of field aiming for stile. Go through kissing gate and follow round right-hand edge of field keeping to immediate left of fence, turning sharp right at outer corner of playing area. Through metal kissing gate at entry to West Buckland and turn left with care onto public road. *West Buckland is slightly larger than East Buckland, and although it has no inn, it does have a small Post Office shop (open mornings only). Its church was, like East Buckland's, re-built in 1860 incorporating a medieval tower.*

Almost immediately turn right at road junction, passing Home Cottage on right and telephone box on left. Bear right at road junction *(but go sharp left if you wish to visit church)*. Pass Gubb's Farm on left as we leave West Buckland on very quiet minor public road.

Barnstaple (see page 55)

This busy but delightful old town, at the head of the Taw Estuary, makes a fitting end to our 102-mile journey from Castle Cary (or our 346-mile journey from Boston!). Despite considerable recent development, much of the largely Georgian centre has survived. For most of its history Barnstaple has been Devon's third most prosperous town (after Exeter and Plymouth) and it has been a great market centre since the Middle Ages. It used to be an important port, although the silting up of the Taw resulted in much trade passing to Bideford.

*Although you are probably anxious, either to return home, or to continue south-westwards on the coast path, do try to find time to visit the interesting Museum of North Devon by the bridge, with its displays including one relating to Tarka the Otter. See also Butcher's Row, a fascinating street with booth-like shops, many of which are still used by butchers, and the Pannier Market, with its great glass roof supported on cast-iron pillars. **There is much more to be seen, but for details consult the helpful Tourist Information Centre at 36, Boutport Street (Tel: 01271 323030).***

Track out of valley beyond Taddiport

(A) Well beyond Gubb's Farm, turn right at road junction (SP - *Taddiport*) and follow road (with sharp turns to right and left) for just over half-a-mile. Road starts to drop more steeply and at entrance to Taddiport down to right, go straight ahead onto roughly surfaced track (SP - *Tarka Trail*). Follow track down into woodlands, then it bends to right and crosses bridge over stream. Beyond bridge keep straight for about 40 yards and then follow track as it bends gently round to right up bank overhung with trees, ignoring gateway to left with tributary stream well over to left. Keep on track as it climbs out of valley, briefly in company with small stream eventually alongside on right. Pass attractive pool on right and just beyond it go straight not left (SP - *Tarka Trail and Gunn*) passing turning on left to Tordown Farm Nature Trail. Large sloping field now visible above to right, but lane still sunken and fields soon visible on both sides.

(B) At end of track, turn right onto minor public road and almost immediately go straight, not left at road junction at Sandick Cross (SP - *Gunn*). We shall now be on public road for about one-and-a-quarter miles; go with care, especially on bends. It is reasonably quiet and there are some fine views over to left through some of the gateways. Pass entry to Sandyke Farm on left. Fork left at Y-junction called Gunn Cross (SP - *Gunn*). On left, pass yard with buildings and possible motor coaches. Pass drive on left to Hutcherton Farm (*not signed*).

(C) Enter hamlet of Gunn passing house called Willowend on left. Turn left with care onto busier road (SP - *Goodleigh*) immediately passing small 19th-century church (*of Holy Name*) on left. About 20 yards beyond church bear left onto very minor road (*no sign*). After passing Cartref on left turn left at road junction onto lane (SP - *Public Bridleway*). *Fine view down to right of the wooded valley towards which we are eventually heading.* Keep on lane past Keeper's Cottage on left and follow lane as it bends to right passing Berry Farm on right. (We shall be dropping down the valley ahead for over a mile.) Fork left at bottom of lane and through gateway. Track now has grass in the middle of it. Through metal gate and turn right down track beyond. Just before reaching metal gate at end of track veer left to go on grassy track with fence and hedge to immediate right. Through next metal gate with bushy area up to left. Track

now has hedge on both sides. Through another metal gate and keep in same direction with sporadic hedge to right and hedge and fence to left. Over small ford on track with woods above to left and track starts to rise. Through large wooden gate and go along top, left-hand edge of field with hedge and bank to immediate left. Fine views ahead and to right. Thatched cottage (marked *Hole* on map) visible over to right on far side of valley. Through wooden gate in fragmentary cross-hedge into next field still keeping to top, left-hand side. Pass wooden gates to left and after about 50 yards go through hunting gate to left of large wooden gate and drop down onto farm roadway at Birch hamlet, passing wooden barn on right and at least one house on left.

(D) Follow roadway as it drops down into valley and pass un-named, white-painted house on left (shown as *Stepfort* on map). Pass entry to Scotts' Clematis Nursery on left - road now public and surfaced. Pass track coming down hill from left and enter pleasantly wooded area with stream visible down to right. Beyond here pass coniferous woodlands to right. Pass steep concrete steps on left leading to Birchwood (bungalow) up to left

Head of valley just beyond Gunn

and then pass its main entrance. Coniferous woods now up to left and then pass forest entrance on right. Pass more woods on right. The smooth flanks of Codden Hill visible well ahead just before bridge carrying busy A361 comes into view.

(E) With A361 bridge ahead, go straight on joining wider road coming in from left (SP - *Landkey*) and then go under bridge (do **not** turn right onto path before going under bridge). Just beyond A361 bridge turn right at road junction (SP - *Harford*) and after about 80 yards turn left over stile (SP - *Tarka Trail*). Head straight across field aiming for stile in cross-hedge to left of power-pole. Over stile and veer left from previous direction aiming for stile at bottom left-hand end of cross-hedge.

Over stile and turn right to walk through Millennium Green, with stream to left and seat on right. Just before end of green bear left to cross bridge over stream. Turn right on edge of football field to go parallel with stream for short distance passing children's

play area on right and veer slightly left to aim for kissing gate beside large metal gate. Turn right onto public road at entry to Swimbridge Newland - *no special features here* - and over bridge crossing stream. Keep straight ahead ignoring roadway to right and cross busier road into Mill Road (SP - *Venn*).

(F) Over bridge crossing Landkey Brook and bear right just beyond by house No. 2 (SP - *Bableigh - Venn*) going up Newland Park Road. Follow road for about 200 yards until it bends to left and after a further 20 yards turn right through large wooden gate (SP - *Tarka Trail*). Go straight across field aiming for stile in cross-hedge. Over stile and along right-hand edge of field with hedge on immediate right. Through large wooden gate and veer right to follow down field with hedge on immediate right. Bear left in corner of field keeping hedge on immediate right and over stile to right of large wooden gate with modern house called *Pendragon* to immediate right.

(A) Join minor public road and continue in same direction going gently down hill. Over bridge crossing the Landkey Brook *(this is the stream that Tarka the Otter came up after being separated from his mate, White-tip, after their fight with ferrets in a timber yard)* and enter Landkey *(see page 53),* its fine church tower being visible straight ahead. Turn left at T-junction below church (SP - *Barnstaple*) *(but turn right if you wish to visit The Ring of Bells Inn - just up to right, on left-hand side, with phone box just beyond).* This widespread village (which also has a shop) has a handsome 15th-century church with a well-proportioned tower and a porch containing a curious roof boss depicting four stags devouring a man's head. The nave and aisles have fine roofs supported on interesting corbel heads, and many charming roof bosses.

(B) Walk up slightly busier road and immediately beyond de-restriction sign turn left off road through gateway onto grassy track between fences (SP - *Tarka Trail*), almost immediately passing transformer on pole. Soon start to drop down into valley with track narrowing to path. Over stile, hedge now on left, bushes and open field up to right. Over stile in tubular steel fence and immediately turn down left to follow winding path through woodlands. Soon curve to right to run parallel to stream not far to left. Soon follow path upwards leaving stream below to left and over stile before turning left **with care** onto public road. Ignore waymark sign opposite and **do not cross road to enter busy and dangerous quarry area**. Go down road with care, first crossing bridge over Landkey Brook and then climbing out of valley beneath fine beech trees.

(C) After about 50 paces turn right off road to go up steep zig-zag path. At top go over possible stile before turning right to follow path leading over bridge spanning cutting between quarries on both sides of path. Then go along field edge with hedge on right. Veer slightly left and soon veer slightly right to join well-defined track. *(Proposed new quarry workings may eventually lead to more route changes - follow possible new waymarks if these route directions become out-dated.)* Soon drop down with good view of Venn Quarries over to right. Follow track as it curves slightly to right and goes downwards passing a two-way fingerpost. Pass woods, first on right and then on both sides and at entrance to large field turn right and very shortly go over stile. Immediately turn left along path between fence on left and woodland on right, ignoring sign on right stating *Footpath via Quarry.* Go along edge of woodlands but be prepared to hear sound of blasting from quarry over to

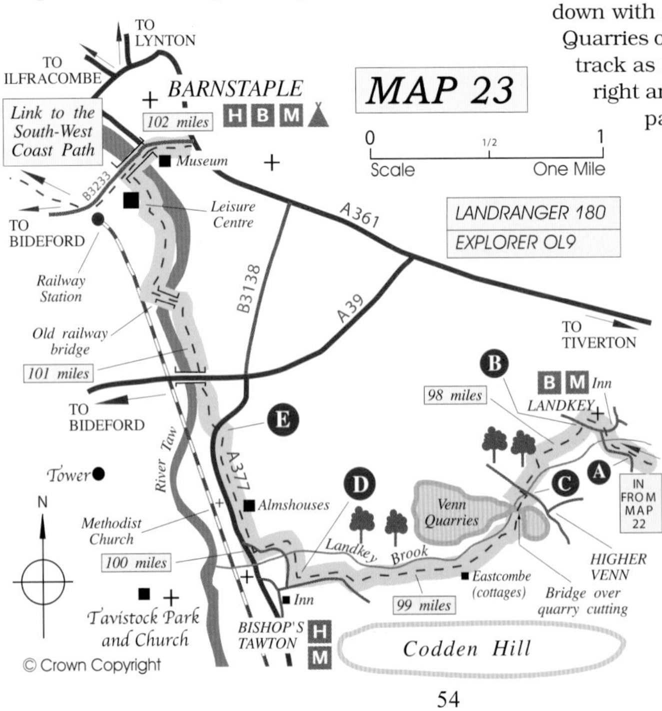

TO LYNTON

TO ILFRACOMBE

+ BARNSTAPLE

Link to the South-West Coast Path

102 miles H B M ▲

■ Museum +

MAP 23

0 — 1/2 — 1
Scale — One Mile

LANDRANGER 180
EXPLORER OL9

Leisure Centre

A361

TO BIDEFORD

B3223

Railway Station

Old railway bridge

101 miles

TO BIDEFORD

B3138

A39

TO TIVERTON

B

98 miles

B M Inn
LANDKEY

Tower ●

River Taw

A377

N

Methodist Church

100 miles

E

Almshouses

D

Landkey Brook

C **A**

IN FROM MAP 22

Venn Quarries

HIGHER VENN

Eastcombe (cottages) Bridge over quarry cutting

■ Inn

99 miles

■ + Tavistock Park and Church

BISHOP'S TAWTON H
■ ■ M

Codden Hill

© Crown Copyright

54

right (any time between 9am and 5pm). At end of wire fence on left start to curve down a little further into wood on much older path, with Landkey Brook occasionally not far to right. Cross slightly more open area and almost immediately go straight ahead over two stiles (SP - *Tarka Trail*) with brook just below to right and Eastcombe (cottages) above, over to left. Cross difficult boggy patch just before going over next stile (if too boggy veer around to right for a few yards). Keep in same direction along wide headland with brook just to right and sloping field up to left. Turn left at far right-hand corner of field and go up to immediate left of hedge for about 30 yards before turning right to cross small stream and go over stile. Follow waymark's direction diagonally up left across field aiming for apparent gap in hedge well below power-pole with transformer, on skyline. Cross boggy patch just before going through gateway in top left-hand corner of field. Keep in about the same direction initially heading for power pole to right of one with transformer. At top right-hand corner of field go over stile beside large gate and bear right onto minor public road. Impressive white mansion well ahead across valley is Tawstock Park. Enter outskirts of Bishop's Tawton going down Sentry Lane. *This large village is strung out along the A377 with a number of old thatched cottages, a pleasant inn and an interesting church. This has an unusual medieval stone spire and there is a 15th-century wagon roof to the nave and several monuments to members of the Chichester family - ancestors to the famous circumnavigator, Sir Francis.*

(D) Turn right, down Easter Street *(but go ahead for a few yards if you wish to visit the Chichester Arms, on left)*. Start to drop down quite steeply and over bridge crossing the Landkey Brook with picnic table on left. Turn left immediately beyond bridge and almost immediately bear left off road to go along track (SP - *Tarka Trail*). At end of track bear left onto public road and go straight down to main road passing *The Sawmills* bungalow on left. Turn right with care onto footway beside the busy A377 *(but turn left if you wish to visit Bishop's Tawton church, which is visible from here)*. When the opportunity offers, cross to left-hand side footway and keep along on it for about three-quarters-of-a-mile. Pass impressive Victorian almshouses on right. Occasional glimpses of tower in trees well over to left beyond River Taw.

(E) Pass telephone box on left of road and where A377 curves decisively to right, bear left down wide tarmac pathway (SP - *Tarka Trail*). Through gateway (gate sometimes completely open) with good glimpse of the Taw to left. Go under massive concrete bridge carrying the A39. Keep on path - now on river floodbank and soon go straight ahead leaving the cycleway/footpath which turns sharp right here. Through metal kissing gate (SP - *Tarka Trail*) onto grassy pathway passing large transformer station on right. Through metal kissing gate beneath old railway bridge and, leaving the Tarka Trail, turn right and right again to go up steps onto old railway embankment. Turn right to cross River Taw on old railway bridge, with good views of Barnstaple down the river to right. At end of bridge turn right onto tarmac path running parallel with river, with tennis courts etc over to left. Go along right-hand edge of large car park with views across river to Barnstaple and ahead right, to its fine 16-arch bridge. Turn right and immediately left to go round right-hand side of large Leisure Centre. At end of pathway, turn right with care to cross bridge on footway into centre of Barnstaple, thereby completing our journey. *(For further information on Barnstaple, see page 51.)* If you wish to link directly onto the South-West Coast Path, turn left and go along the B3233 for about 500 yards to turn right, opposite the Railway Station entry - and good luck with the rest of your walk! **If you feel like supporting Macmillan Cancer Relief it would be very much appreciated. See page 4 for details.** But whatever the outcome, do drop us (Peter & Janet) a line - our address is on the title page.

INDEX